D1476007

Wm Jackson

More
Dakota
Mysteries
&
Oddities™

by Wm Jackson

Published by
Valley Star Books, Inc.

Dedication

This book is dedicated to the memory of **The Valley Star** newspaper which published from May 5, 1993, to June 7, 2000. **The Valley Star** did what's rare for small town newspapers by reporting the truth instead of acting as a public relations representative for powers-that-be. We consider **The Valley Star** newspaper the mother of Valley Star Books, Inc. May the offspring promote the truth as well as the newspaper did.

A VALLEY STAR BOOK

First printing, 6000 copies - August, 2000

ISBN softcover: 0-9677349-2-4
ISBN hardcover: 0-9677349-3-2

Copyright ©2000 by William Jackson

Dakota Mysteries & Oddities is a registered trademark
Published by Valley Star Books, Inc.
P.O. Box 309
Velva, ND 58790

All rights reserved. No part of this publication may be reproduced in any form or by any means without the prior written permission of the author.

All photographs, unless otherwise noted, were taken by William Jackson or Arlyce Forthun-Jackson

Printed in USA

FOREWORD

One of the most interesting men to ever live on the prairie was the Marquis de Mores. Known for his meat packing scheme in Medora, he was better known, in France, for his dueling. Just how many men did he fight? How many did he kill? Did he kill a man while in North Dakota? Was his meat packing scheme part of his dream to become France's next emperor?

Then there's Kate Richards O'Hare's story. Although Red Kate had given her speech several times without incident in other states, when she spoke in Bowman in 1917, she was arrested for sedition. Sentenced to five years hard labor, her political opponents thought this stint in jail would forever quiet what they considered her dangerous socialistic preaching. Were they ever wrong!

You might become outraged when you read Ed Wormsbecker's story. Can you believe this 74-year-old man was evicted by McHenry County authorities because he was delinquent to the tune of $108 in back taxes. Of course this happened long ago, didn't it? Something like this couldn't happen in these times! Check the story's date. It was 1999. Read how the courts reduced this senior citizen to the ranks of the homeless.

One of the most touching stories in this book is about brave Shelley Wiersch's fight against the crippling symptoms of multiple sclerosis. In a brave attempt to get her life back, she endured upwards of 20 bee stings a day. Her courage in the face of a life of debilitation, is an enduring lesson for all of us.

Once, again, my wife Arlyce and I visited the Fort Ransom area where we tracked down the notorious writing rock and a mooring stone. Could it be that lay historians are correct when they claim that Writing Rock is a message in an ancient Sino-Tibetan alphabet? Is that stone, with its three-and-a-half inch hole, a mooring stone gratis an inland trip by the Vikings?

I ask you to take a break from our mundane world and engross yourselves in the stories in this book. Who knows, your life might never be the same!

William Jackson

TABLE of CONTENTS

Only the baby survived

John Kraft thought it odd there was washing on the line when he drove by Jacob and Beatta Wolf's farm three miles north of Turtle Lake. There's no way those clothes were going to dry on that cold, muggy day. Besides, the garments were in disarray as if they'd been tossed around by the wind. So, Kraft stopped at the house and called out, but nobody answered.

Hearing unusual pig grunts, he turned his attention toward the barn. When he opened the door, he found the heinous sight of Jacob Wolf and two of his daughters, Maria and Edna, lying dead on the ground with bullets to their heads.

Kraft closely checked out the house where he found drops of blood leading to the basement's trapdoor. Downstairs he discovered the bodies of Jacob's wife, Beatta, daughters Bertha, Lydia, and Martha, and Jacob Hofer, the

Hundreds of mourners attended the funeral for eight held at the Wolf farm three miles north of Turtle Lake. Baby Emma is the baby behind her mother's casket, second from left. All eight were, buried beside each other in a family plot at the Turtle Lake Cemetery. The monument reads Die Ermordete Famielie, which in German means the murdered family.

- photo courtesy Emma Wolf Hanson

Hundreds milled about the Wolf farm on the day of the funeral.　　　-photo courtesy Emma Wolf Hanson

13-year-old hired hand. The victims had either been shot or bludgeoned to death with a hatchet.

Someone had murdered every single member of the Wolf family except for nine-month-old baby Emma who lay in her crib in a small bedroom.

The medical report concluded the family was murdered two days earlier on April 22, 1920.

Less than a month later, Henry Layer, a neighboring farmer, confessed to the murders. He said he'd gone to the Wolf farm demanding damages for their dog's attack on his cow. Rather than pay up, Layer said Wolf grabbed a double barreled shotgun and loaded it.

"I then tried to take this gun away from (him) and in the fight. . .one shot went off and then another in quick succession," Layer confessed to police. "One of the shots killed Mrs. Wolf. I didn't see her fall, but saw her lay there. I then got the gun away from Wolf and, then, got more shells out of the bureau drawer in the front room. . .I reloaded the gun and began shooting."

"I shot at Jacob Wolf who, by this time, had run out of the house across the yard towards the cow shed. . .I saw Jacob Wolf fall. I then. . .fired another shot into Wolf's body. I then went into the cow shed (where I saw) Wolf's two girls and shot them. . .I then returned to the house and there shot

and killed the rest of the Wolf family."

"The reason I did not kill the baby was, I believe, because I did not go into the room (where) the baby lay."

Layer was convicted of murder and sentenced to life with hard labor and no parole. So ends the tragic story, or, does it?

One year later, Henry Layer, claiming his confession was made under duress, asked for a new trial. The request was denied.

Four years later, on his death bed following an appendectomy, when asked if he was the Wolf family killer, Layer reputedly said, "My eyes are guilty, but my hands are free of their blood." Does that mean he watched as the murders were committed by somebody else?

Consider Layer's statement about not killing the baby. Remember, he said, "The reason I did not kill the baby was, I believe, because I did not go into the room (where) the baby lay." Why not? Surely the baby was awake and screaming following the loud sounds of repeated shotgun blasts? Wouldn't a man intent on killing everyone who could identify him have checked every room in the house just to make sure no one survived?

Consider the doctor's report after he examined Baby Emma. He said the infant was fed between the time of the murders on April 22nd and the discovery of the bodies on the 24th. Did Henry Layer, or, somebody else feed the baby?

10

Then there's the two masks John Hofer claims his children found while playing in a clump of bushes "about sixteen steps east of the Wolf house." This family lived on the farm just after the murders. That November, Hofer said his children not only found the masks but, also, a 12-gauge black shotgun shell and a woman's blood stained dusting cap.

Finally, there's the feelings that have haunted Emma Wolf Hanson, the surviving baby, for the last 80 years. Of course, she doesn't know what happened on that fateful day that changed her childhood forever. Over the years, she's tried to put the puzzle together based on what others have told her.

"He was found guilty, and he died in prison, but I have suspicions. How could one man kill everybody?" she asks. "I think he was protecting his family."

Could this survivor's strong convictions about the murders be even stronger than one man's, later recanted, confession? Emma's been told when she saw Henry Layer at the funeral, she screamed. "Of course, I don't remember," she says.

One of the most mind boggling events of this story reputedly happened at the funeral for the eight victims that was held on the Wolf farm. The story goes that Layer asked that the coffins be opened so he could look at the deceased. In front of 2500 people, he looked into each victim's face though several had none left. To this day there are those who ask "Why did he do this?"

TODAY

Emma and her husband Clarence celebrate their 60th anniversary on September 29, 2000. They reside in Turtle Lake, just a few miles from her family's homestead. Emma's lived in that community all her life except for the few years she resided in Washburn.

She was raised by her mother's only sister, Christina Hofer, and her husband Emanuel. "To me they were mom and dad." However, for a few weeks, when Emma was a first grader, the Hofers' custody was challenged. The sheriff came and got her while she was writing at the school blackboard.

- photo courtesy Emma Wolf Hanson

Seeing this, Walter Hofer, two-years older than she, ran almost a mile to tell the family "they'd gotten Emma." After a two-week battle, she was returned to the Hofers, and they continued raising her with their 12 other children. Today, only Walter and Emma are left of the family. Although Walter is in California, they keep in touch. "I consider him my brother," Emma says.

"I feel very sad that I've had to be without a mother and a father." Every Memorial Day, when Emma visits the eight graves buried in the cemetery just north of Turtle Lake, she's filled with remorse that her little sisters were killed with an ax.

Devils Lake

Skyline Skiway

Patterned after the Lake Placid ski jump, Devils Lake's Skyline Skiway was popular with Olympic skiers. Built in 1932, the 118-foot slide with a 38 degree slope was set atop a 200-foot hill.

Local skier Peder Falstad made the first jump, a leap of 190 feet, on inaugural day, December 31, 1932. Minot's Casper Oimen, also, jumped that distance that day. Oimen was captain of the U.S. Olympic team at Lake Placid of which Falstad was a teammate.

A few months later, Falstad - the Central United States' ski champion - set a new state record off Skyline Skiway.

The jump was closed in 1938. Although many similar jumps were built around the state to accommodate Scandinavian skiers, few of them remain today. Gone is the Fargo jump which was touted as the longest in the state.

Belcourt

The Virgin Mary tree

Almost every morning for the past six years, James and Patricia LaFountain, rural Belcourt, have sat at their kitchen table drinking coffee. Invariably they look out to enjoy a nearby grove of trees or, maybe, young rabbits hopping about. However, on March 30, 2000, Patricia says she saw something totally different in this natural Turtle Mountain setting. She says she saw the image of the Virgin Mary.

"I called my husband. He came out and looked at that oak tree. He spotted the image right away. He said, 'I can't believe this. It's a miracle.'"

Patricia swears the optically converging branches forming the outline of the Virgin Mary holding a baby weren't there before that morning. "It was just an ordinary tree," she contends. Whether the tree has undergone a miraculous transformation or not, it's certainly no longer considered "ordinary."

Over 2000 flocked to the site within the first week turning the LaFountain's back yard into a mound of muddy footprints. A priest saw the image right away and told the LaFountains to string blue and pink lights around it. On April 1, 100 people gathered to say the Rosary and share a brunch. Women knelt in the grass and mud.

"I believe the image is a message," Patricia says. "People are killing too much. They're beating each other up. There's domestic abuse, and they're on drugs. I think it's a message for people to start straightening up and believing."

Others believe too. Flowers, ribbons, and rosary beads, including a strand from Italy, have been draped on the tree. Hundreds of snapshots have been taken. It's been reported when some of the photos are developed, other images appear. A man said one of his photographs shows a more defined image of the Virgin Mary behind the tree. A woman claims the image of St. Joseph standing off to the side appeared on one of her photographs. Others reported seeing halos and the image of an Indian woman in their pictures.

Can you find the image of the Virgin Mary holding baby Jesus? This photograph was taken just outside the window of the LaFountain's kitchen. If you can't make out the image, follow the string of lights.

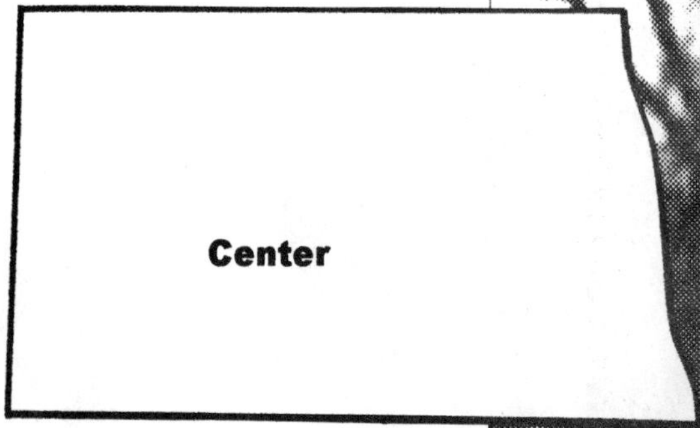

Center

In Center there's a granite shaft that stands in tribute to Hazel Miner, the 16-year-old girl who perished during a blizzard. Miner is credited with saving her younger brother and sister after the threesome was lost on their way home from school on April 11, 1904.

When the relentless fury of the blizzard let up, rescuers found Emmett and Myrdith huddled under the outstretched body of their sister.

In
Memory
of
HAZEL MINER
APRIL 11, 1904
MARCH 16, 1920

To the dead a tribute
To the living a memory
To posterity an inspiration

THE STORY
OF
HER LIFE
AND OF
HER HEROIC
TRAGIC DEATH
IS RECORDED
IN THE
ARCHIVES OF
OLIVER COUNTY
ON PAGES 130-131
BOOK II
MISC RECORDS

STRANGER READ IT

Jamestown

The man without a country

For two-months in 1999, Hussen Mohammed sat in a North Dakota jail because he was a *man without a country*. For the past 20 years Mohammed had lived in Canada. Then, in September, 1998, while bird watching on a rural road, he accidentally pedaled his bike into northern Minnesota. He was stopped and charged with illegally entering the United States.

An immigration judge ordered the errant cyclist returned to Canada or to Somalia, his homeland. The problem is Canadian officials won't accept Mohammed's reentry because he served six months after being charged with marijuana possession in 1998. Authorities suspected he intended to distribute the drug. Mohammed contended the marijuana was his own personal stash that he used to ease the pain of a bad burn he'd suffered in 1997.

Off to Somalia, then? Not yet anyway. That area's in political turmoil with no central government. Besides, Hilima Siad - Hussen's mother in Toronto - contends her son doesn't know that country's language or culture and he's not Islamic, which some contend, would threaten his life.

That leaves one country, the United States, where the country-less man could settle. Evidently that's not going to happen either. Once Mohammed was convicted of drug possession with intent to deliver, he became persona non grata for admission to this country.

Finally, last February, after 18 months incarceration in a dozen or so facilities, Mohammed was released and housed in a Minnesota home. His mother said he was hoping for gainful employment. Despite that possibility, he remains a man without a country. At any time he faces the threat of deportation to Somalia.

Hussen Mohammed was housed in the Stutsman County Jail in Jamestown from January - March of 1999.

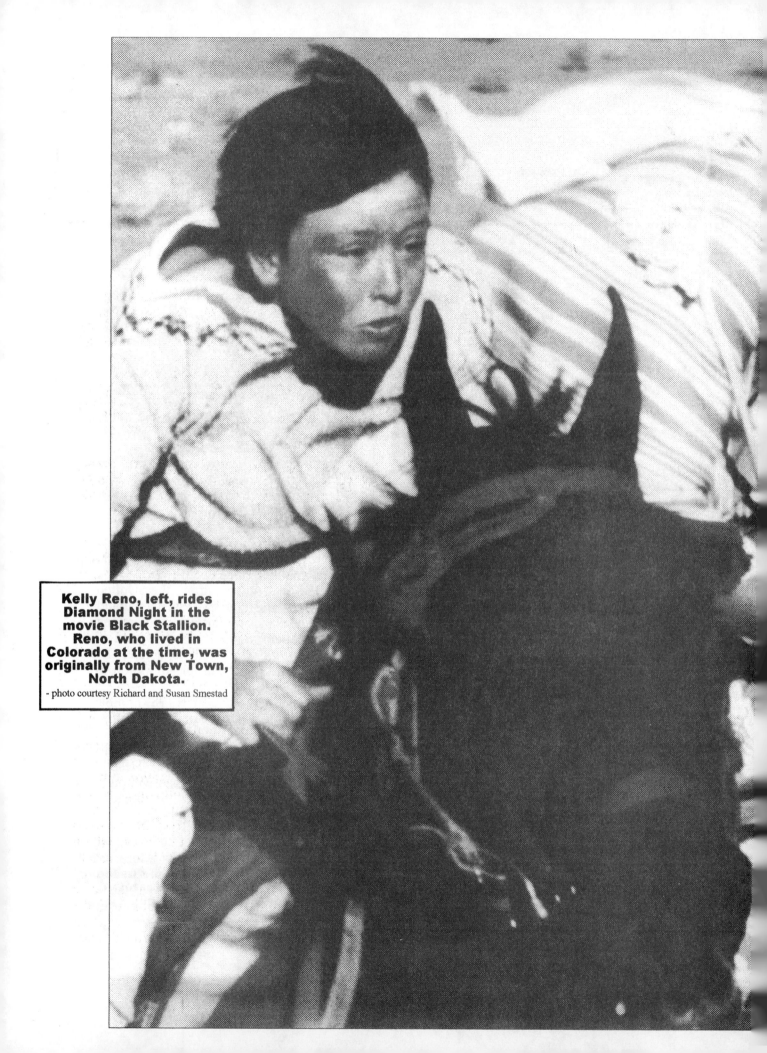

Kelly Reno, left, rides Diamond Night in the movie Black Stallion. Reno, who lived in Colorado at the time, was originally from New Town, North Dakota.
- photo courtesy Richard and Susan Smestad

Harvey

North Dakota's miracle horse

Diamond Night, a horse raised on the Richard and Susan Smestad ranch near Harvey, was cast as Shetan in the 1981 movie **The Black Stallion**.

The United Artist release, produced by Francis Ford Coppola, was the first of a series of movies based on the books by Walter Farley published in the 1940s. Farley insisted a real stallion be used in the film. "He didn't want Lassie on the Hoof," explained Susan. "He wanted something true to the spirit relationship of animal with the boy." That was a tall order because only one percent of Arabian stallions are black and stallions generally have a temperament that's earned them the reputation of being bulls in the horse world. "You normally don't put children with stallions," she said.

After checking out horses at many ranches, Diamond Night was chosen because he was a true black stallion with a gentle disposition. The Smestads took him to California for training.

The choice turned out to be a good one as the horse learned his tricks and temperamentally fit in with the demands on the set. On the screen, he was a sensation meaning more movies were planned. Then

Black Night had an accident that, perhaps, gained him more notoriety than even his stardom in the movies.

While training, he was cued to rear. He came down awkwardly and twisted his left front leg. With a loud crack, the leg broke in nine places above the elbow.

Although veterinarians urged the horse be put down as soon as possible, the owners just couldn't bring themselves to do that without trying to mend Black Night's devastating injury. But how?

A cast wouldn't work because of the location of the fracture. A bone plate couldn't be used because the break was too near the elbow.

A unique plan was proposed. It was decided to insert horizontal pins through the leg and bone, then hold the pins in place with an *external* vertical pin called the Kirschner-Ebner device. Although this procedure had been used on small animals, it hadn't been tried on animals nearly as large as a horse.

A machinist was brought in to make a large device suitable for the large patient. Within a few hours, an entire crew completed the device and the surgery was performed. The key to the success of the procedure, though, was if the horse could be kept quiet enough to heal.

Newspapers across the world honed in on this heart retching story. As it turned out, the operation was successful, and Black Night led a full life offstage, dying at the age of 18 in 1994.

Grassy Butte

Grassy Butte's Sod Post Office

Donald McKenzie built this adobe covered log building in Grassy Butte in 1914. For the next 50 years this sod roofed structure served as the local post office. McKenzie and his wife were the first owners and operators followed by James Warren. Grass continues to grow from the roof in what is now a local museum.

Dakota roads

North Dakota State Highway 46 is touted as the longest stretch of road in the state without a curve. This straight highway runs 113 miles from just west of Hickson to just east of Streeter. Though there are a few minor curves, highway 46 is, for the most part, as straight as an arrow.

North Dakota has more miles of roads and streets per capita than any other state in the nation. There are 167 miles per 1000 population.

The longest state highway is North Dakota 200 which stretches 309 miles. The shortest is the .4341 mile long state highway 91 at Harvey.

The longest national highway in the state is US 2 which runs 354.99 miles. The shortest is I-194 which is only 1.0538 miles.

Pictured is state highway 46 west of Kindred

Information from the planning and programming division of the North Dakota Department of Transportation

Drake

She fights MS with bee stings

Would you let your spouse sting you with honeybees 20 times a day, three times a week? Shelley Wiersch does.

This unusual family activity which began in October of 1997 is, actually, therapy for multiple sclerosis.

Shelley, rural Drake, learned about using apitherapy (bee-venom therapy) while watching the TV show **Unsolved Mysteries**. On the program, MS sufferers described how good they felt after being stung. Some told how they were able to throw away their wheel chairs and canes. Shelley wanted to try it.

Diagnosed with MS 12 years ago when she was just 22, Shelley used conventional treatment for years to control a numbness in her legs. However, her condition worsened until she couldn't use these limbs anymore. Since starting apitherapy, she's felt sensations. "I can feel something when I scratch my thighs," she says. She's even been able to reduce the dosage of the conventional drugs she takes.

The Wiersches follow charts to direct the placement of the sting. Shelley's husband, Barry, picks up each individual bee with a long tweezers and holds it on a trigger point until the bee stings his wife.

"When the bees cooperate, he can administer the usual 20 stings in five to 15 minutes," Shelley says.

She well remembers the first stings to her neck. "It's good I couldn't reach my husband's ear," she says. "I would have ripped it off, it hurt so bad!"

After months of bee stings, Shelley says the pain isn't as intense, and the welts are much smaller. "It only burns for one or two minutes," she says.

Anna, a friend and nurse, claims Shelley's eyes are clearer, and she's more vibrant. Her moods are better, too.

When she had to go without bee stings for a week-and-a-half because of an area shortage, she had a setback. "I noticed a great loss. . .I couldn't feel my thighs when I scratched them," she says. To keep the

22

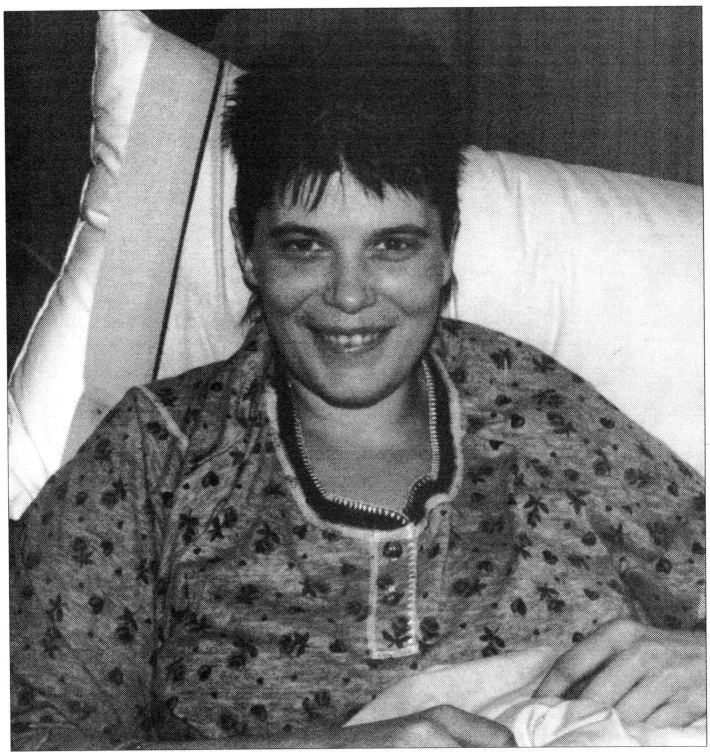

- Photo by Gini Rostad

supply constant, they, now, order the bees by mail.

Despite the successes, there are times when Shelley wants to quit the program. She says she tries to adopt her nurses' philosophy to celebrate the little things until the big things come. Although she has a twice-weekly housekeeper, she cooks meals and does some daily chores. She uses a wheel chair to get around her home. To relax she reads romance novels and mysteries.

However, Shelly yearns to enjoy the outdoors and go for rides with the family. She wants to be around the cattle on the farm. The best she can do, now, is watch her husband and 12-year-old son Travis from the window. "I haven't been able to touch my horse yet. I, finally, got a paint horse. I've wanted one all my life," she says.

Maybe bee sting therapy will make it all happen for her.

Author's note: The original version of this story by Gini Rostad appeared in the April 1, 1998, issue of *The Valley Star* newspaper. Tragically, Shelley Wiersch died a few weeks later from causes unrelated to the bee stings.

Casselton

The Rags to Riches Governor

He was orphaned when he was four. Still a kid, he joined the Union Army as a drummer boy. He survived the war to become governor when he was only 32. Is this the plot of an upcoming Hollywood movie? If so, they'll have to promote it as a true story.

Andrew Burke was born to Irish immigrants John and Mary Burke on May 15, 1850. Life was hard from the beginning as his mother died in childbirth. Four years later, Andrew's father died leaving the youngster to become a ward of the Children's Aid Society. When he was nine, he was boarded onto an Orphan Train and sent to live on a farm in Noblesville, Indiana.

He had to beg his foster guardians to allow him to run off to become a Civil War drummer boy. After the war, he returned to his Indiana farm home and saved up for two years of college.

In 1880, along with his Minneapolis wife, he moved to Casselton, North Dakota, with just $65 in his pocket. He took a job as a bookkeeper for a general store. Then he became cashier of a local bank. After serving three terms as the Cass County Treasurer, he ran in the state's gubernatorial election and won.

Ten years after Andrew Burke came to this state with just $65 in his pocket, he was elected governor!

Four Casselton governors

Those driving by Casselton, today, can't miss a billboard on the interstate boasting the town as the home of four governors. Of course, there's Burke. Then there's William Langer, who was elected the state's 17th governor in 1932 and, then, re-elected again a few years later. They, also, claim William Guy who was, actually, born in Devils Lake. However, Guy went to school and farmed near Amenia, the town directly north of Casselton. He served as governor from 1961 to 1972. The last Casselton governor, so far, was George Sinner who served from 1985 until 1992.

Andrew Burke

William Langer

William Guy

George Sinner

State Historical Society of North Dakota

Governor trivia

- North Dakota's 5th governor, Frank Briggs, was the first governor to die in office. He succumbed to tuberculosis in 1898.

- John Burke, the state's 10th governor, was nicknamed "Honest John Burke" because of his campaign against corrupt business practices. Later in his political career, Burke served as U.S. Treasurer for many years. A monument in his honor was dedicated at the nation's capitol in 1963.

- Louis Hanna, 11th governor, went to Norway to present that country with a statue of Abraham Lincoln. Later, Norway decorated him with the Grand Cross of St. Olaf of the First Rank.

- Lynn Frazier, 12th governor and the first Nonpartisan League candidate elected to that office, was ousted by his party's own reforms. Pushed by the NPL, the legislature had passed a public recall amendment to the state constitution. Ironically, in 1922, Frazier was among the first recalled! However, the next year he was elected to the U.S. Senate, a seat he held till 1940.

- It wasn't until Walter Maddock was elected the 15th governor did the state have a native son at the helm. He was born in Grand Forks, Dakota Territory in 1880. He served in office from 1928 to 1929.

- Thomas Moodie, the 19th governor, has the distinction of serving the shortest term in office. Shortly after his January 7, 1935, inauguration, it was learned Moodie voted in Minnesota about three-years earlier. Eligibility rules required those seeking the gubernatorial spot to live in this state for five consecutive years before the election. He left the state's top spot after just five weeks.

- One of the reasons John Moses, the state's 22nd governor, was so popular was because he gave his speeches in English, German, or Norwegian depending on the ethnicity of his crowd.

- All but four of the state's 30 governors were born in this country. Those who weren't include Roger Allin, the 4th governor, born in Devonshire, England; Ragnvold Nestos, the 13th governor, born in Voss, Norway; Walter Welford, the 20th governor, born in Belley, Yorkshire, England; and John Moses, the 22nd governor, born in Strand, Norway. The last eight governors were all born in North Dakota.

Information acquired from the Governors of North Dakota exhibit produced by The State Historical Society of North Dakota that toured the state.

Bowman

Woman jailed for her views

Some historians mark July 17, 1917, as the state's darkest day in civil rights. That was the day authorities arrested a woman for speaking out against the nation's involvement in World War I.

It wasn't the first time Kate Richards O'Hare told audiences that American mothers were raising their sons for fodder in what was becoming a very unpopular war at home. Fact is, Red Kate, the name she'd been dubbed because of her socialist views, had delivered the speech 75 times before at gatherings across the country.

However, after she gave her speech to a packed audience in Bowman, she was arrested and charged with sedition, a new crime the country enacted with the 1917 Espionage Act.

Few predicted O'Hare would be found guilty at her trial in federal court in Bismarck. Little did they know that an out-of-state judge who supported the war effort would be brought in to oversee the proceedings. O'Hare was found guilty and sentenced to a five-year stint of hard labor at the Missouri State Penitentiary beginning in 1919.

Although military organizations across the nation applauded O'Hare's incarceration, most Americans were appalled that a mother of three was jailed for exercising her freedom of speech.

A group, led, in part, by O'Hare's husband Frank, campaigned nationwide for her release. Many historians say that group was the forerunner of the American Civil Liberties Union. Their efforts were successful.

Just over a year after she was jailed, O'Hare was released. She immediately took up where she'd left off and began speaking across the nation. This time, though, she was armed with stories about atrocities within our prison system. She published two books, **America's Prison Hells** and **In Prison**.

Along with her husband, she organized a march on Washington demanding amnesty for political prisoners. Her own rights were restored by President Calvin Coolidge.

Towner

A day late and a dollar short

To some, Ed Wormsbecker's home, just north of Towner, was nothing more than an old, dilapidated mobile home. To Ed Wormsbecker, it was his one-acre paradise, bought and paid for with hard, honest sweat.

All this is in the past tense because Wormsbecker's home is no longer his. In June of 1999, the 74-year-old man was evicted by McHenry County because he owed $108 in property taxes!

"I'm a lifelong resident of this area. I'm not a tax protester," Wormsbecker said. "I want to make that clear. I'm no Gordon Kahl."

Maybe he isn't Gordon Kahl. However, it's obvious Ed Wormsbecker is a man of strong convictions. He said he let his taxes slide while waiting for county tax officials to personally inspect his property. He thought the taxes on his mobile home, which are separate from the property taxes, were too high. He was told to take the matter before the county commission.

However, in Wormsbecker's mind, that wasn't a plausible solution. He'd once had a row with the then county board chair and,

now, didn't think he'd get fair treatment. So, he planted his feet to ride out the pending storm.

Wormsbecker called me, a reporter at the time, to the scene to wait for the police on eviction day. We sat in his living room while the clock ticked down the final 30 minutes before the tidal wave hit. During that time, Ed told his story.

He explained how he'd put in a good septic system that cost $3200. He was proud of the new windows he was about to use to replace old ones. These aren't those cheap trailer windows, he said, pointing to the windows he'd never get to install. "They've got wood frames."

Wormsbecker was especially proud of the large table saw in his living room. He felt comforted about his new furnace which could well outlast him. Then there were all his woodworking tools! All of these, soon, could belong to another man.

That other man was Terry Dewitz, the local deputy sheriff, who purchased the property from the county for back taxes. Actually, Dewitz hadn't purchased the trailer, just the land. If Wormsbecker had

Carrying his cat, Ed Wormsbecker is greeted by his dog as a
deputy sheriff escorts him from his home north of Towner.

only removed his mobile home and contents before the clock struck noon, he could have kept his personal property.

Unfortunately, this simple solution wasn't an option because Wormsbecker owed around $450 in back taxes on his trailer. He could move the trailer only if he paid these past due taxes. Although that seems a pittance to most, it was a lot for Wormsbecker who only gets that much in a month from Social Security and SSI.

So, Ed Wormsbecker sat back in his chair while the clock on a table to his right ticked away the minutes. Just before noon I said to him, "Ed, you've got just five minutes."

"The clock's a little fast," he said somewhat matter-of-factly.

Nonetheless, just as the big hand struck 12, Wormsbecker stretched his neck to look out the window as a car drove up. "The big guy himself is here," he said referring to the county sheriff.

Wormsbecker answered the pound on the door. The sheriff and a deputy came in and seemingly filled the small living room. They asked Wormsbecker if he was ready to leave. He said he'd decided to defy the court order because this was his home.

The sheriff, then, instructed his deputy to return to Towner to get instructions from the judge. Although Wormsbecker told the police that I was his guest, I decided to wait outside. A human element had crept into my thinking. Just moments earlier, in true John Wayne fashion, Wormsbecker made it clear to me that he wasn't voluntarily leaving his home. I knew his defiance could cost him dearly. However, if that was his choice, I respected it. I just didn't want him to feel he had to continue his stand to prove a point to me.

Outside, I positioned myself to get a good photo of Ed Wormsbecker walking out the door on his own, or, being dragged out by the police.

Over an hour passed before the deputy returned with orders from the judge. A little more time slowly ticked away before Ed Wormsbecker, carrying his cat and a few articles of clothing, walked out the door. He was eagerly greeted by his big black lab.

Almost apologetically he stopped for a second, looked at me, and said they told him he faced a year in jail and a thousand dollar fine if he didn't leave.

Wormsbecker and his animals got into his old car and drove away.

Towner residents split on the eviction. Some said the old man got what he deserved. He hadn't paid his taxes, so, he paid the consequences. Others felt bitter that the county evicted a senior citizen for a paltry $108. Some pointed to the fact that Wormsbecker did bring in the money after he received a demand letter from the county. The problem was he didn't meet the 30-day deadline.

"We got the money together for him," said daughter Candy Lee Wormsbecker. "He would have had it in on Friday (the final day), but I didn't get paid till Friday afternoon." So, on Monday, Ed Wormsbecker took the money to the courthouse, but they wouldn't accept it.

I was unable to find Ed after his move. About three weeks later, I tracked down family members. Carol Wormsbecker said he lived out of his car for about a week and a half. "He'd park along the river or at the race track. Now he's living in an old camper trailer out at my aunt's," she said. "There's no electricity, no heat, nothing." Life was, essentially, a camp-out every night.

Carol said she was more than just concerned about Wormsbecker's physical well being. "Emotionally, he's very upset," she said. "He always kept himself busy, always making something, building something. He loved to bake. He had a big garden. He loved to read. He kept himself occupied all the time." Now, he barely has a roof over his head.

A couple months later, with winter just around the corner, county social services, after receiving a call from Senator Byron Dorgan, found an apartment for Wormsbecker. He moved 45 miles away to Velva where he, now, lives in an apartment complex for the elderly and disabled.

The really odd twist to the story is that the man who bought the property from the county with hopes of moving onto it, resigned from the police force just a couple weeks after the eviction for an out-of-the-area job. A year later the old Wormsbecker residence remained vacant.

Ed Wormsbecker tells his story just moments before he was evicted from his home for $108 in back property taxes.

North Dakota
South Dakota

The Dakota Quartzite Border

China built the Great Wall to isolate their culture from the barbarism of the outside world. The Soviet Union's Iron Curtain was a political wall that led to the Cold War. The 49th parallel between Canada and the U.S. became the location of border crossings. Albeit of less renown, North and South Dakota's boundary is defined as the Quartzite Border.

In 1891 the first 800 pound quartz marker was set near the intersecting corner of North Dakota, South Dakota, and Minnesota. Other markers were, then, set at one-mile intervals to the west until a physical border existed between the two newly formed states. In all, 720 markers were permanently put in place.

Although some of the markers were moved over the years, most are still firmly embedded in Dakota soil today. Some call these red-stone markers the silent sentinels on the prairie.

The lichen covered marker, right, located near Hettinger and Haynes is numbered 289. Deeply inscribed into the quartz on the north side of the marker are the letters ND, on the south side are the letters SD. Although sunk deeply into the prairie sod, 109 years of frost has still caused the marker to lean off to the side.

Williston

Williston's marauding postal fleas

There was a time in the 1930s when the Williston Post Office was flea infested! According to Bill Shemorry, a retired newspaperman of 64 years and, now, local author, the post office received several boxes of coyote pelts that were to be shipped out parcel post. In order to weigh the pelts, postal employees loaded them off the back dock and rolled them in on a cart. One box fell off and broke open.

Out hopped thousands of little red fleas. It didn't take the fleas long to find the clerks. One poor soul ended up covered with thousands of the pesky critters.

The unlucky man stripped and bathed in a downstairs shower. Still, he was infested with biting marauders. The story goes he ended up taking several kerosene baths.

The boxes of pelts were placed back on the loading dock. That night the temperature dipped to 25 degrees below zero. The next morning, postal workers found thousands more fleas had crawled out of the boxes and frozen to death on the dock. It was said they looked like red confetti.

For more information on this story and other stories from the Williston area, read the *Best of the Best Little Stories.* **Address inquiries to Bill Shemorry; P.O. Box 33; Williston, ND 58802-0033 or call 701-572-3380**

Bill Shemorry poses with a caricature sketch of a postal flea.

The Shawnee murders

A lot of people from the Larimore-Niagara-Shawnee area sighed when they heard that poor ole Eugene Butler died at the state hospital in 1911. Butler's unusual antics were well known. Just before he was committed in 1903, he'd started riding his horse at 'break-neck speed' around the countryside.

Frequently he'd arise from his night's slumber, grab the revolver he kept under his pillow and check out his house for intruders. He'd often saddle up and ride about his property looking for culprits.

Some thought it was Butler's lifestyle that drove him to lose his senses. He'd come from New York state in 1880 and settled on three quarters of a section of land. He built a comfortable home. Despite all his successes, though, he mostly kept to himself. Locals regarded him as a hermit and a miser.

The doctors at the Jamestown asylum noted Butler's unusual behavior. They wrote in their reports that he was haunted by hallucinations that someone was after him. Then there was his fear that if his photograph was ever taken, he'd die.

So, when Eugene Butler did die so died a troubled soul. As it turned out, it was four years later before anyone knew just how troubled this man's soul might have been!

It was in 1915 when Leo Verheulehn was digging a cellar under Butler's old house and discovered bones. Authorities determined the bones were human skeletons. What's more, they discovered this burial site was beneath a hole that had been cut in the floor of the room directly above.

Rumor got around quickly that there were six human skeletons buried beneath Eugene Butler's house. Tongues wagged when it was revealed that five of the skulls had been split open as though by a blow from a dull object.

The first theory that circulated was that Butler had killed some of the transient farm laborers he was known to hire.

The second theory was that the skeletons were those of an elderly man, two housekeepers and their children. Suspicions were that Butler had killed some of the housekeepers he'd employed over the years. He had, occasionally, been overheard saying he'd fired housekeepers and told them to leave. Had he really not fired them but killed them?

Now, almost a hundred years later, no one really knows for sure just how those bones got there. Was Eugene Butler so crazy that he'd savagely killed six people and, then, buried them under his house? Or, as some suspected, was it all business with him. Did he let his workers tally large wages on the books before he whacked them on the head instead of paying them?

Butler's house remains to this day as does the mystery of who killed whom and why.

Hove Mobile Park

State's smallest city

The state's smallest *incorporated* city is Hove Mobile Park with a population of two. Although over a hundred people once walked the town's streets that have since been plowed under, husband and wife Howard and Marion Hove, are the last remaining residents.

The Hoves built the park in a field across the road from their farmstead in 197O when the government ordered the building of an anti-ballistic missile site seven miles to the west.

Howard said they only planned on running a trailer court on what was once a wheat field. However, in 1972, after over 100 settled there, he soon learned they needed a way to solve people problems. So, the trailer court was incorporated as a town with official meetings held in the Hove kitchen. Voting booths were set up in their den.

During its heyday, the community boasted all the amenities of any small town. The Hoves built a state-approved sewage lagoon. Good soft, water was pumped into the trailer court from a well dug by Hove's grandfather who homesteaded there in 1884. The city's annual $800 budget was mostly used for snow removal. The school bus stopped to haul kids off to the Langdon district.

Then people left Hove almost as quickly as they came when the missile site unexpectedly closed in 1976. That saddened the remaining residents most every morning when they went to get the mail from their rural boxes.

Marion remembers when she got a call from Philadelphia from a fellow who wanted to set up a doughnut shop in Hove. "I kept telling him we only had a population of two," she said. Still he continued his pitch. Finally, she stressed there were only two people in town. Whereupon he said they must have a bad connection and, immediately, hung up.

Then there was that letter from some elementary students in Portland, Oregon who wanted to know more about such a small town. The letter was addressed: Any Citizen; General Delivery; Hove Mobile Park, ND. Although Hove never had a post office, the letter still found its way to Howard and Marion's rural Fairdale mailbox.

What's Hove's future? "Every year when I do my annual report, we consider dissolving, but we decide to continue another year," Marion said. Besides it's just possible the town will boom once again. There is talk of the country setting up another missile defense system, isn't there?

Just one mailbox remains on the rural route that runs by Hove Mobile Park. The park proper was located across and up the road past the grove of trees. At one time over a hundred people lived there. Although an incorporated city, the state refused to provide the little community with a standard highway sign. Marion and Howard Hove, inset, are the last two residents of the paper city. Howard acts as mayor while Marion serves as auditor. Every year they sit at their kitchen table to decide if they want to continue doing the paperwork that gives them the distinction of not only being the smallest city in the state, but one of the smallest in the nation.

Dakota's biggest fish

North Dakota's biggest fish dates back to the days of the dinosaurs! The monstrous paddlefish that can tip the scales at 200 pounds and the pallid sturgeon, that often weighs 70 pounds, swam our waters while dinosaurs walked our shores. Both fish can be found, today, still swimming in the Missouri and Yellowstone Rivers.

PADDLEFISH

Some consider paddlefish the continent's most unique species of fish. They feed on plankton and aquatic insects by weaving their long paddle-like snouts back and forth seemingly honing in on food. Some scientists believe their snouts have sensory organs that help them locate food sources. The theory that these fish rely on an ancient electrical sensory perception system spawned a U.S. Department of Defense study.

As is the case with primitive fish, the skeleton of the paddlefish is made up of cartilage rather than bone although they have a few bone structures in their jaws.

These large gray-blue fish, often sporting white undersides, can be found in water channels. Their skin is smooth like that of a catfish.

PALLID STURGEON

Pallid sturgeon, also, employ a unique method for finding food. They rely on barbels that dangle from their chins to find fish and invertebrates. These barbels, similar to those on catfish, are extra sensory organs. They use them to scour the bottom of the river in search of food which they suck up in their toothless mouths.

Instead of scales, sturgeons have bony plates. Like other ancient fish, their skeletons are made up of cartilage. Although pallid sturgeon live up to 50 years, they've found themselves on the endangered species list with only an estimated 250 still in North Dakota waters in 1998.

It was decided, then, to release 750 pallid sturgeon into the Missouri and Yellowstone rivers to stave off their extinction.

MORE JURASSIC ERA FISH

Also, in North Dakota waters, are shovelnose sturgeon that weigh in up to five pounds. Hybrids of the pallid and shovelnose have been found in waters further south. Then there's the lake sturgeon that was re-introduced into the Red River system by the Minnesota Department of Natural Resources.

Source: U.S. Fish and Wildlife Service and N.D. Game and Fish Department

This paddlefish, top, and pallid sturgeon, bottom, are actually graphite replicas housed at the North Dakota Game and Fish offices in Bismarck. Some experts believe paddlefish are the continent's most unique species of fish. Pallid sturgeon, bottom, are on the endangered species list.

Lake Sakakawea Records

In the warm winter of 1999-2000, Lake Sakakawea didn't freeze over until January 16, breaking the record set 13 years earlier by a day.

Records kept since 1953-54 show the lake as freezing over 33 times in December compared to 11 times in January. Twice the lake froze over in November.

Spring thaw came at a record, too. Lake Sakakawea was officially declared ice-free on March 31, 2000, one day earlier than the 1990 record.

Of course these two records lead to the lake's third record for the season as it was frozen over for just 75 days. The previous record of 79 days was set while the lake was filling during the winter of 1954-55. Oddly enough, the following winter the lake was frozen for the longest time, 165 days.

Hiddenwood Cliff, across Hiddenwood Creek, was an ancient landmark for buffalo-hunting Indian tribes who often camped in this valley. It was here and within a 30-mile area in 1882-83 that the American buffalo made their last stand.

Hettinger
Haynes

State's last great buffalo hunt

Lt. Colonel George Custer and the 7th Cavalry camped at the base of Hiddenwood Cliff on July 8, 1874. They were led here by Indian scouts on their way to look for gold in the Black Hills. The camp held 2000 men, 1000 cavalry horses, 900 mules, 300 beef cattle, and 150 wagons.

The town of Hettinger in southwestern North Dakota boasts on billboards that it's the site of the last great buffalo hunt in the state. The hunt actually began, on June 20, 1882, to the northeast on Hiddenwood Cliff, not far from Haynes. It continued past Hettinger as a massive herd of 50,000 buffalo attempted to elude 2000 pursuing Sioux hunters.

The Sioux were in ecstasy because they thought the great buffalo herds, that had fed and clothed them for generations, had returned. Little did they know that of the millions of buffalo that once roamed the plains, this was but one of two large herds left. The other had broken off and taken a route into Montana.

Over a three day period at Hiddenwood Creek, Sioux braves, using repeater rifles as well as bows and arrows, killed 5000 of the great prairie beasts. The herd scattered. Over the next couple of years, reports came from other areas of kills of these stragglers. However, the day of the big herds ended with the Hiddenwood Cliff hunt and similar hunts of their Montana brethren.

It was in 1883 when president-to-be Teddy Roosevelt came to the Badlands to hunt buffalo. He was shocked there were only a few scattered herds left. Now, little mounds of bleached bones had become a much more common sight than the buffalo themselves.

At one time an estimated 75 million of these massive beasts with bulls weighing upwards of a ton roamed across the Dakota grasslands. While in the Dakotas, Lewis and Clark recorded seeing 52 herds from a single vantage point. The clock of change sped up with the arrival of another massive beast, the Iron Horse. The fate of the buffalo was sealed.

When the Northern Pacific went through, it cut off the herds to the north and the south. White hunters rode the rails. Their ensuing parties killed all the buffalo within a day's ride of either side of the tracks. Further commercialization doomed the prairie's most formidable animal.

This early day KTHI-TV 11 postcard touted their tower as the Western Hemisphere's highest man-made structure. With the fall of the tower in Poland, their tower is now the tallest man-made structure in the world.

photo courtesy KVLY-TV

America's
Tallest
Tower

FARGO • GRAND FORKS

World's tallest towers

Blanchard
Galesburg

The world's two tallest towers are in North Dakota. The tallest, KVLY-TV's 2063-foot tower, reaches skyward near Blanchard. KXJB-TV's tower, at 2060 feet, is located near Galesburg. Although KVLY's tower is the tallest from base to top, KXJB's actually stands higher because it's on ground that's 70 feet higher above sea level.

Both towers are taller than the Eiffel Tower at 1056 feet and the Empire State Building at 1472 feet. Both towers are taller than the combined heights of the Great Pyramid Khufu at Gizeh, the Eifel Tower, and the Washington Monument.

KVLY's tower was, originally, built as the KTHI tower. Those call letters stood for **The HIgh** tower! For awhile the tower could only boast that it was the continent's highest manmade structure until the slightly higher television tower in Poland fell to the ground in the '70s opening the door to the worldwide claim.

KVLY put together these facts about their tower:

The tower and guy anchors take up 160 acres of space. - There are 14 levels of light on the tower, seven levels are flashing code beacons spaced 300 feet apart. - The antenna on top of the tower is 113 feet high and weighs 9000 pounds. - In a 70 mile per hour wind, the beacon light on top of the tower moves approximately ten feet. - If an iron worker on the antenna dropped his wrench, it would be traveling 250 miles per hour when it hit the ground.

KXJB's tower was, actually, built three times! Less than two years after it was first constructed in 1966, a Marine helicopter struck it and crashed, killing the four aboard.

The accident caused the tower to crash into a twisted heap of metal, bolts, and cables. An engineer on duty at the time, was uninjured although a portion of the roof and one wall was crushed. Five months later a new tower at the same location was operable.

Then, on April 5, 1997, this rebuilt tower crashed following a severe wind and ice storm that ravaged the eastern part of the state. Again the building sustained considerable damage. The roof, two walls, and the heating and cooling systems had to be repaired. No one was at the transmitter site at the time.

LARGEST AND LONGEST BROADCAST
The longest live television broadcast in the state's history took place on July 4, 1989, when the KX network (including stations in Bismarck, Dickinson, Fargo, Minot, and Williston) broadcast the "KX Party of the Century" to celebrate North Dakota's centennial. Programming was from 6 a.m. to midnight with a laser light show on the state capitol building as the finale.

Niagara

The man with the most space debris?

William McManus, Niagara, claims he has the most space debris in the world! For the past ten years he's been collecting and trying to identify what he saw fall to earth on November 20, 1989.

Around 1:00 a.m. on that morning, McManus was driving home after completing his snow plowing shift. He watched a large ball of fire light up the night sky. The glow from that ball was so bright he picked out area farmsteads.

An air force retiree, McManus calculated the hurtling object landed about five miles away. His search for debris actually took him to fields about 20 miles away. Then, in March of 1990, he hit pay dirt when he spotted what looked like green rock

sticking out of a ridge. The ridge was part of the old Lake Agassiz shoreline.

McManus dug up the six-by-eight-inch rock and, gratis Superman, dubbed his find kryptonite. Over the years, he found about 250 pounds of green rock, ranging from fingernail to fist size, not only buried in the ridge but, actually, lying atop the grass.

At first he thought what he'd found was a meteorite. However, no experts confirmed his beliefs. One claimed the find was volcanic rock called basalt. Another thought it was either that or industrial slag. But, McManus asked, where's the volcano that blew out this basalt or the factory that smelted the slag? Remember, he pointed out, he found some of the rock atop the

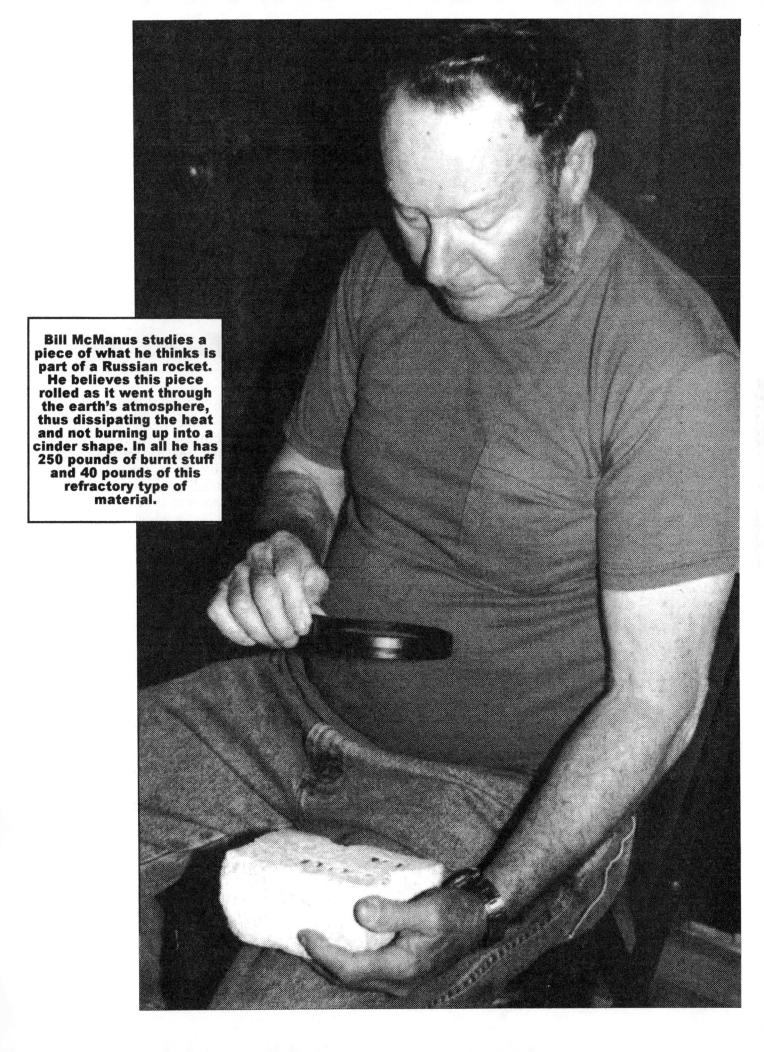

Bill McManus studies a piece of what he thinks is part of a Russian rocket. He believes this piece rolled as it went through the earth's atmosphere, thus dissipating the heat and not burning up into a cinder shape. In all he has 250 pounds of burnt stuff and 40 pounds of this refractory type of material.

McManus thinks these letters indicate part of the rocket was made in Germany.

earth's surface.

Seven years and several thousand dollars later, McManus was told by the Colorado Assaying Company in Denver that the samples he sent were conglomerate rock or andesite lava rock containing mostly silicon. Other major metals found in the samples were aluminum and iron with traces of calcium, magnesium, titanium, and zirconium.

This information discounted McManus' belief that he'd found a meteorite. However, he still didn't buy the basalt/industrial slag theory. Spending more time and money, he pursued another angle and contacted the North American Aerospace Defense Command. Specifically, he wanted to know if a rocket or satellite re-entered the earth's atmosphere on November 20, 1989.

The answer was that the body of Soviet Union rocket The Kosmos 2049, launched on November 17, fell to earth somewhere in the northern hemisphere on November 20.

McManus' mind clicked - northern hemisphere, North Dakota - could it be one and the same? Could the "meteorite" he saw plummeting to earth actually have been part of that Soviet rocket?

Not so fast. The Johnson Space Center added another piece to the investigative puzzle. They told McManus that debris from the U.S. rocket Thor Ablestar, launched in 1961, also re-entered the earth's atmosphere on November 20, 1989.

Now McManus was torn between two possibilities. He'd scrapped the meteorite theory. He'd chucked the basalt/slag theory. However, he knew what he saw on that night when that blazing spheroid fell to the earth. And he knew what he found on that ridge. Could what he'd found been part of a Soviet rocket, or, was it part of an American satellite?

After weighing the two theories, McManus concludes his find was the bits and pieces of a Russian SL4 rocket motor that burned up as it plunged to earth.

Although the final verdict isn't in yet. McManus has found inscriptions on what he thinks is the brick lining of the Soviet rocket. The letters he's found, so far, include: **.P.GROZZOUIA**. One source told him these inscriptions discount the Russian rocket theory because there is no letter "G" in their alphabet. "I have a friend in Russia who is checking on this spelling," McManus says. Additionally, he thinks parts of that rocket could have been made in Germany.

In the meantime, William McManus continues digging on both that ridge for more fragments and around the world for the truth about his find. You can see the light in his eyes when he exclaims, "I've got the most space debris in the world."

Minot

'Oldest House in North Dakota'

The Sigdal House is touted as the Oldest House in North Dakota. Located in Minot's Scandinavian Heritage Park, the 230-year-old building was originally built around 1770 in Sigdal, Norway. The house was purchased, dismantled, and shipped to Minot where it was reassembled. Dedication was on October 15, 1991.

The oldest building actually built in what is, now, North Dakota, and still standing is the Kittson Trading Post near Walhalla. It was one of two buildings constructed in St. Joseph in 1851 by Norman Kittson, agent for the American Fur Company. In 1904, visionary historians salvaged one of the trading post buildings which had become stables for the Bellevue Hotel. The building was dismantled and rebuilt on a nearby hill which became the Walhalla State Historic Site.

For more information see Dakota Mysteries & Oddities™

Powers Lake

Man won't sell $400,000 rock!

Wilburt (Bud) Smith, Powers Lake, won't sell a rock that might be worth up to $400,000. Smith suspects the rock is the 1910 meteorite that landed about six-and-a-half miles southwest of Bowbells near his Uncle Ike Ross' farmhouse in 1910. In an old newspaper article, Ross described the meteorite as a ball of fire descending from the heavens.

The meteorite reportedly smashed through the side of a sod shack and embedded itself two-feet into the earth. There Ike found the four-pound stone which he kept until he died in 1914. Over the ages, the rock was passed down to two of Bud's uncles.

In 1936, one of the uncles told the, then, eight-year-old Smith that the rock fell from the sky. For several years it had been used as a doorstop.

Geologists have wanted to test the rock to determine if it really is a meteorite. Smith's not that interested. He's lugged that heavy rock around with him even when he was in the army and during six moves since 1936.

"It maybe is worth nothing. I don't know, and I don't really want to know," Smith said. As far as he's concerned, knowing if the stone is worth millions or nothing would put an end to this fascinating story. Right, now, he isn't ready to write the final chapter.

> Over the years Smith has become a rock hound in his own right as he's collected hundreds of rocks. He said when the last glacier came down from the north, the Powers Lake area was as far as it came. "It kept melting as it came," he said. "It was like a conveyor belt. It dumped these rocks in my field. I've hauled them all my life. Whenever I see an odd one, I pick it up."

48

Is the rock, pictured above with the holes in it, a meteorite that fell in 1910? Bud Smith, right, thinks it might well be the meteorite that landed near his Uncle Ike's farmhouse near Bowbells. The rock has been passed down through the generations. In 1936, an uncle told Smith the rock fell from the sky. For several years it was used as a doorstop.

Photos courtesy Bud Smith

Great Northern Railroad's Worst Wreck

Thirty-four people died when two trains collided near Michigan on August 9, 1945. Among the dead were 19 servicemen on their way home. It was the worst wreck in the history of the Great Northern Railroad.

On a curve of track just west of Michigan, one train broke down for the third time between that town and Larimore. Unaware of the delay, the second train rounded the curve and plowed into the last car of the first train.

Balta

The center of it all

Arlyce Forthun-Jackson, the author's wife, second from left, and her mother, father, and sister, stand at the sign and point to the real geographical center near Balta in 1992.

For years tourists have flocked to a stone cairn in Rugby to see the geographical center of North America. Many have had their photos snapped as they stood by a sign that reads: **Geographical Center of North America - Rugby, ND**.

It's a great tourist attraction that draws many roadsters off U.S. Highway 2. The only problem, according to some rural residents, is that Rugby isn't the real center of the continent. The real center, they claim, is located not too far from the much smaller community of Balta.

Locals there say the real center is located six or seven miles west of Balta in the middle of what some call Voeller Lake. Others have renamed this mudhole American Lake or Geographical Lake. One resident simply says the center is located in what he calls the Lake Around the Curve.

According to the story, about 1931, geologists came to the area and determined a spot in the lake bed was the true center. Then, about 20 years ago, locals took advantage of an iced up lake and dumped eight or nine truck loads of rock over what they thought was the true center. They, then, topped the location off with an American flag.

Since then the flag has weathered away to nothingness. Rising waters now cover the rocks. For the most part, just a few straggling tourists ferret out Balta's geographical center each year while thousands stop by Rugby's

In December of 1992, the author's daughter, son, and wife attach a flag to the pole atop the rocks dumped by locals marking the true geographical center.

Just who is correct? Is the center of North America really in Rugby as the sign says, or, is it really isolated in a lake bed west of Balta?

Karen Mitchell, a geologist with the state geological survey, says the colloquial description is, probably, the right one. She said the real center's latitude is 48 degrees 10 minutes north with a longitude of 100 degrees and 10 minutes west. Rugby's is latitude 48 degrees 22 minutes north with a longitude of 99 degrees 59 minutes west.

That puts the center about 25 miles from Rugby, or, just about smack dab in the middle of that lake.

Although there's usually water in the lake, there have been dry periods allowing easy access to the continent's true geographical center. Perhaps an upcoming dry time will mean the geologic marker can be found. It should be there because the real center has been used as a base for geodetic measurements.

However, undertakers of this project might have a little difficulty if all that rock they hauled in covers up that marker!

In the meantime, area Balta residents think it's okay for tourists to visit the cairn in Rugby. They just wish someone would put up little markers pointing the direction to the real center so that geologic purists can find the true center of it all.

When you get your photo snapped in front of Rugby's cairn, you are *almost* at the geographical center of North America. The actual center is near the little town of Balta to the southwest.

Bottineau

Honk, Honk!

Drive down Bottineau's main street, and you'll find Ole's Auto sporting a sign that reads *Hometown Friendly Service*. Invariably, inside the stalls, mechanics work on vintage automobiles and *only* vintage automobiles.

Drive down main street a few months later and, believe it or not, those same vintage rigs are still in Ole's garage. Slow mechanics? Not really! Ole's Auto is a fantastic 3-D mural painting on the side wall of the town's local newspaper.

During the spring and summer of 1998, Pam McLean, Peggy Lider, Robin Williams, and Carlette Kamrud graphed a chalk outline and slapped on 25 gallons of paint after using block filler to smooth out the stucco wall. To "build" Ole's brick building took 700 hours of labor.

North Dakota's Killer Twisters

The state's most deadly tornado system killed ten people as it spawned five twisters that cut a 27-mile wide path of destruction. One of those funnels ripped up 100 blocks of a residential district in Fargo. Ten people died including six members of one family. One-hundred-three people were injured.

Although North Dakota isn't in *Tornado Alley*, the state averages 18 tornadoes a year. Of course, some twisters that touch down might never be seen in sparsely populated areas. In 1976, 56 twisters ravaged North Dakota plains.

According to the National Weather Service in Bismarck, the state averages one F-5 (winds ranging from 261 to 318 mph) twister every 15 years, one F-4 tornado (207-260 mph) ever 6.5 years, one F-3 (158-206 mph) every 19 months, two F-2 (113-157 mph) per year, five F-1 (73-112 mph) per year, and 11 F-0 (40-72 mph) per year.

State Historical Society of North Dakota

A Fargo man dejectedly walks through the rubble of what's left of his home after an F-5 tornado ravaged the Golden Ridge area, on the northwest side of town on June 20, 1957.

Figures show that the state actually has as many tornadoes reported as Arkansas. However, that state has many more killer twisters. North Dakota had eight killer twisters since 1956, Arkansas recorded 56.

Besides tornadic winds, North Dakotans have to put up with strong gusts and straight line winds. According to the National Weather Service, the following counties recorded winds of 100 miles per hour or more from 1980-99. Slope: 143, Grant: 128, Ward 119, Williston 113, Kidder 110, Stark 105, Stutsman 102, and Emmons, LaMoure, Morton, Parker, and Trail all at 100.

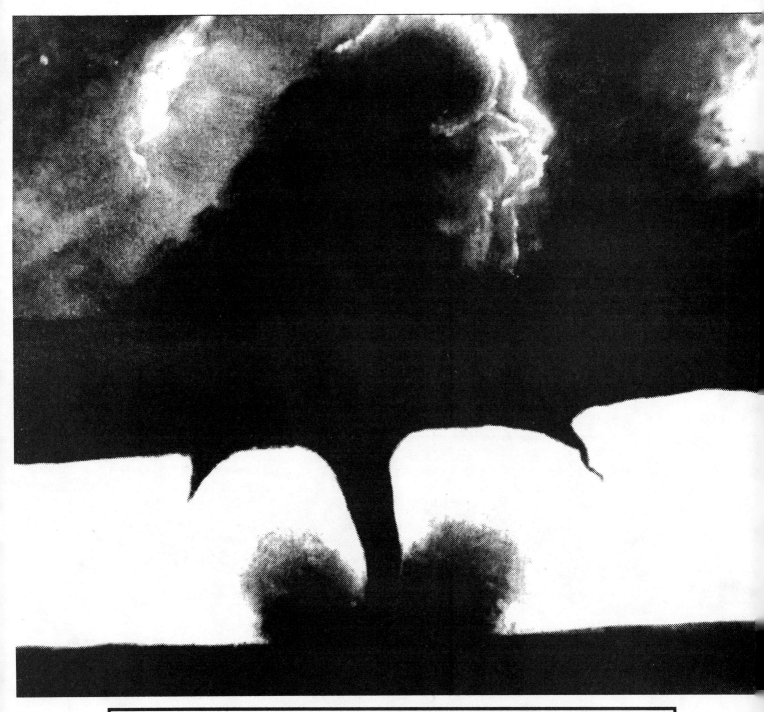

- photo by F.N. Robinson, courtesy State Historical Society of North Dakota

Sister twisters develop from this ominous looking August 28, 1884, tornado photographed in Miner County, Dakota Territory.

From 1950 to 1994, there were 799 reported tornadoes in North Dakota causing 22 deaths, 288 injuries and billions of dollars of damage. Although an average 18 twisters touch down in the state each year, 56 pounded the prairie in 1976.

It should be noted there could be more tornadoes than reported. Tornadoes touching down in sparsely populated areas could go unnoticed.

Map of North Dakota showing: Olga, Williston, Mondak, Dogden Butte, Grand Forks, Schafer, Weller, Steele, Williamsport, Wahpeton

Hung by the neck till dead!

Charles Thurber has the dubious distinction of being the victim of the first known lynching in what is, now, North Dakota. On October 24, 1882, a mob of 2000 broke into the Grand Forks jail, dragged Thurber off, and strung him from a railroad bridge that crosses the Red River.

Thurber, a black man, was accused of assaulting Minnie Traska, an immigrant girl, near her farm home. While fleeing, some say he assaulted another woman.

Details are sketchy. It's been argued that one accuser later recanted her story, and that Thurber was a victim of race rather than a criminal.

Less than two years later, on the morning of June 23, 1884, **Jack O'Neil,** aka Jake and Tom, was found hanging from a tele-graph pole at Six Mile Coulee, about two miles northwest of Weller. He'd been hanged by his own lariat.

Evidently, O'Neil was well liked by many. When word got out about his hanging, some speculated he'd been throwing his lariat in the air when it caught in the pole with the lower end accidentally twisting around his neck. Others rumored he committed suicide.

However, a local newspaper reported he died with his boots off and his hands tied behind him. They reported rumors of two rewards totaling $1400 that were offered for the suspected horse thief.

Cowboy historians still argue whether O'Neil was a good guy or a bad guy.

In November, 1884, eighteen cowboys

identifying themselves as members of the Box L Ranch in Montana, allegedly rode into Dakota territory and tracked down three suspected horse thieves named **Ravenwood**, **Baites**, and **Gardepee**. Although one witness said he later saw the accused being hauled back to Montana to stand trial, others claimed they were either hanged or shot east of Dogden Butte, near the current town of Butte. The lyrics of a ballad handed down over the years claim the three were hanged on November 6. According to local legend, that following spring, three skeletons were washed ashore at nearby Strawberry Lake.

In late 1885, **Louis Olson** aka Louis Gunderson was lynched in Olga which was, at that time, Cavalier County's largest town. Olson was accused of beating Susan McEwen to death at her homestead shack near Rosa Lake.

Four special constables were sworn in to take Olson to Pembina jail. However, before they left, wagon loads of angry Rosa Lake residents pulled into town. A local newspaper reported hundreds of people had assembled when the mob jostled Olson from the clutches of the law, put a rope around his neck, and dragged him from the hotel door to a grove of trees where they hanged him.

On July 27, 1888, 100 determined men from Wahpeton and Breckenridge, overpowered the sheriff and 12 deputies and lynched Deputy Sheriff **Lee Elmer** for allegedly killing Mollie Korbel, the county jail's maid.

While the mob beat at the door, Elmer quickly tied a cloth noose, hung it over his head, and tried to jump off his cot. The suicide attempt failed, and the mob fastened his hands behind him and dragged him along the streets to the bridge that spans the Boise de Sioux between Wahpeton and Breckenridge. Here he was trooped around a thousand people who'd come to watch. Then he was hanged off the bridge.

According to old newspaper accounts, just before the lynching, when asked if he had anything to say, Elmer answered, "No. Nothing I could say would save me now. I killed the girl, and I am sorry. I was crazy when I did it."

In a newspaper interview following the lynching, the Wahpeton sheriff said he and his deputies offered all the physical resistance they could. However, he said, he decided to not shoot nor fight because the mob was all his friends and the life of the murderer wasn't worth their lives!

On November 14, 1897, three Indians were lynched at Williamsport, the now defunct county seat of Emmons County.

Earlier in the year, six members of the Thomas Spicer family were killed near Winona. Five Indians - **Alex Coudot**, Frank Blackhawk, George Defender, **Paul Holy Track**, and **Philip Ireland** - were arrested for the crimes.

Tried singly, Coudot was convicted in district court. However, the state supreme court reversed the conviction. Angered by this legal action, a mob dragged Coudot, Holy Track, and Ireland from the Williamsport cell and hanged them.

According to a newspaper account of the day, E.S. Allen, the prosecutor, said after the hanging, the vigilantes started toward Bismarck where Blackhawk and Defender were housed in the Burleigh County Jail.

"They had proceeded as far as Mandan when they decided to stop at a resort and get a drink," the article reported Allen as saying. "The leader of the mob. . .after having been given a drink of whiskey, snatched up a glass containing ammonia and, thinking it to be water, swallowed it at a gulp. The shock to his system was so great, he fell to the floor dead."

According to this account, the mob, "lacking a leader, lost most of its venom and gradually dispersed." Charges against Blackhawk and DeFender were later dropped.

If justice had been allowed to take its course, Holy Track and Ireland, both youth, would have escaped the hangman's noose because they had agreed to testify against the three older men.

In November of 1912, fifty angry mob members battered down the Kidder County jail door, dragged off **George Baker** and lynched him from a pole in Steele's

58

stockyards. While he dangled in the air, three bullets were fired into his body.

Baker was suspected of shooting to death his estranged wife Mabel and her father Thomas Glass while they were at Glass' home in Dawson. Officials found seven bullets in Mabel who, supposedly, was trying to escape through a window.

Typical in lynching cases, the police did little. According to a newspaper account, the sheriff said every man in the crowd was from out of town. It was, also, reported that no cemetery in the county would accept Baker's body.

In April of 1913, **J.C. Collins'** clothes were set afire after he was hanged from a telegraph pole near Mondak. Collins, allegedly, killed a sheriff and deputy who'd come to arrest him after a minor disturbance.

Sheriff Thomas Courtney and Deputy Sheriff Richard Burgmeister of Sheridan County, Montana, went to the Union Bridge Company three miles west of Mondak to serve a warrant on Collins who was part of the gang building a railroad bridge over the Missouri River.

Shortly after the hanging, the body disappeared. Some thought members of the lynching party tossed Collins' remains in the river to destroy any evidence.

On December 17, 1913, drifter **Cleve Culbertson** was lynched in Williston after he'd received a life sentence for murdering Dr. D.A. Dillon, his wife, and their 12-year-old daughter two months earlier. According to accounts, a mob of 40 or 50 used a 14-foot watermain pipe to batter down the county jail's door, seized Culbertson, loaded him into an automobile, and drove to the Little Muddy River bridge where they hanged him. When they cut him down, officials found Culbertson's body riddled with eleven rifle bullets.

On January 29, 1931, **Charles Bannon**, the last person lynched in the state, was hanged from a highway bridge in the now defunct town of Schafer. This was 16 years after capital punishment was abolished in the state.

A 22-year-old farm youth, Bannon moved onto the Albert Haven farm near Schafer. He told locals that the Havens asked him to take care of the place while they were away in Oregon. A few months later, Bannon was charged with embezzlement when he tried to sell some of the Havens' hogs. When authorities searched the farmstead, they found five bodies buried in the barn.

Bannon admitted he murdered the family. However, he said his father James Bannon who was, also, living on the farm, wasn't involved.

Fearing a lynching, authorities housed Bannon at Williston's county jail. When they moved the prisoner back to Schafer facilities to await arraignment, their fears came to pass.

An estimated 80 masked men drove up in 16 autos and two trucks. They overpowered police officers, then battered down the jail doors. They bound Bannon and dragged him along a road for about two miles where they hanged him off a highway bridge over Cherry Creek, his body plunging twenty feet.

Newspaper accounts reported Bannon died pleading for his father's life. The mob spared him, but the courts didn't. James Bannon was convicted of first degree murder and was sentenced to life imprisonment. Released on September 12, 1950, Bannon told reporters he was innocent. "I was railroaded into it," he said.

Although there are no records, it's thought suspected horse thieves were lynched in the early days. It's interesting to note that never in the state's history has any member of a lynch mob been prosecuted!

STATE LYNCHINGS

1882 - Charles Thurber - lynched - Grand Forks
1884 - Jack O'Neil - suspected lynching - Weller
1884 - Ravenwood - suspected lynching - Dogden Butte
      Baites - suspected lynching - Dogden Butte
      Gardepee - suspected lynching - Dogden Butte
1885 - Louis Olson - lynched - Olga
1888 - Lee Elmer - lynched - Wahpeton
1897 - Alex Coudot - lynched - Williamsport
      Paul Holytrack - lynched - Williamsport
      Philip Ireland - lynched - Williamsport
1912 - George Baker - lynched - Steele
1913 - J.C. Collins - lynched - Mondak
1913 - Cleve Culbertson - lynched - Williston
1931 - Charles Bannon - lynched - Schafer

Fargo

Who hit the most homers?

Although Mark McGwire and Sammy Sosa eclipsed the single-season home run records of both Babe Ruth and Roger Maris, there's still talk around the Fargo area about which of these two great sluggers of the past *really* had the best season.

Of course, George Herman Ruth AKA Babe, the Sultan of Swat, and the Great Bambino, was one of the greatest sluggers of all time. He was, also, a good pitcher in his early years. While on the mound he won 94 games while losing only 46. He pitched 17 shutouts and chalked up an ERA of just 2.28. However, it was what he could do with his monstrous Louisville Sluggers, some weighing over 50 ounces, that has forever endeared him in the hearts of baseball fans. Yankee Stadium became known as the "House that Ruth Built." Most thought that the Babe's record of 60 home runs set in 1927 would forever remain on the books.

That's why there were hostilities when a relatively young unknown lad from North Dakota closed in on that record 34 years later. As fate would have it, Roger Maris never fit in with the Good Ole Boys who secretly, and sometimes openly, rooted for Ruth.

An all around athlete, Roger Maris was a standout football player for Fargo's Shanley High which earned him a recruitment to the University of Oklahoma. He had a chance to play under the Sooner's famed Coach Bud Wilkinson. But Maris didn't like it there, so, he quit after a couple of weeks. Shortly after, in 1953, he signed to play professional ball for the Fargo-Moorhead Twins. He was a good, all-around player. But he wasn't a home run king, yet. He hit just nine home runs in 114 games.

The following year, while playing for Keokuk in the Three-I League, Maris demonstrated home run potential by belting 32 over the fence in 134 games. He was major league bound.

During his rookie year with the Cleveland Indians in 1957, he banged 14 home runs. He then played for Kansas City. In 1960 he was traded to the Yanks and landed a spot in right field. That season he blasted 39

Roger Maris' baseball achievement is commemorated on the monument at his grave site in Fargo. Maris hit 61 home runs in 1961 causing some to exclaim he beat Babe Ruth's record *against all odds*.

homers. The always pennant hungry Yankees were impressed with Maris' bat.

Then came the famed 1961 season when Yankees Roger Maris and Mickey Mantle battled, much like McGwire and Sosa, to break the home-run record. As recorded, Mantle's bat came up short while Maris' made the history books. He'd beaten the Sultan of Swat!

However, the beloved Bambino's record wasn't broken without controversy. As the race heated up, baseball commissioner Ford Frick ruled that Maris had to break the record in 154 games, not in the new 162 game season.

"You can't break the 110 meter record in a 100 yard dash," Frick said.

"A record is a record. You think anybody is going to care how many games it took?" Maris retorted.

It was in the fourth inning of a game with Boston on October 1, that Maris launched the shot that broke Ruth's record. He did it, but he didn't do it in 154 games.

Maris did make the history books. However Ruth's name was still there, too. Asterisks were used to denote Maris held the 162 game home-run record while Ruth held the 154 game record.

So, the real record holder remained the talk of the barber shop until McGwire's bat awed the fans 37 years later. Putting that recent pinnacle aside, let's resolve **once and for all**, mathematically, who really had the best home-run season, Ruth or Maris?

Ruth hit 60 home runs in 154 games. That's a homer for every 2.57 games. Maris hit 61 home runs in 162 games, or, a homer for every 2.66 games. Mark an X for Ruth.

Wait a minute. Maris didn't hit his first home run until ten games into the season. So, he really hit 61 home runs in 153 games, or, a homer for every 251 games. Mark an X for Maris.

Look at it another way. Ruth officially batted 540 times. Maris officially batted 590 times. So, Ruth hit a home run every official nine times at bat. It took Maris 9.67 trips to the plate to pound the big one. Mark an X, then, for Ruth.

Hold on. Their *actual* appearances at the plate were nearly equal. 692 for Ruth, 698 for Maris. That means Ruth hit a home run on the average every 11.53 trips to the plate. Maris hit a homer every 11.44 turns at bat. Mark an X for Maris.

Tally this mathematical accounting and, guess what, they're both tied again! Nothing's settled. There's only one thing to do. Toss the matter back into the barber shop arena!

In the meantime, Ruth has the distinction of making Baseball's Hall of Fame. Maris. didn't make it because, it's argued, he only had a couple great years.

Although you won't find Maris in the hall, you will find the ball there that he belted out as home run number 61.

A Day to Remember

November 24, 1993 will long be etched in the minds of the Joe and Theresa Keller family of Velva. On that day, Joe and Theresa marked 50 years of marriage. Also, on that day, their daughter Sandy Erck, Garrison, received a phone call from the Nashville Network's Tenth Anniversary Contest telling her she'd won $10,000. "I entered the contest by sending in four postcards with my name and address on it," Sandy said. Also, on that day, another daughter, Gerry Brekke, Grand Forks, received a call from Home of Economy telling her she'd won a new pickup. "When I put my registration in the box, it was so full I had to stuff it down into the box. I thought, fat chance!" Gerry said. The story goes that another daughter, Karla, Grand Forks, upon learning about the family's good luck of the day, rushed out and bought some Minnesota lottery tickets. Alas, the luck had run out, Karla wasn't a winner!

Carrington

State's last World War I vet

- photo courtesy Marvin Baker

One-hundred-four-year-old Otto "Ole" Ihringer, North Dakota's last World War I veteran, died December 11, 1999, in Carrington.

In the fall of 1918, he spent 70 consecutive days in the trenches fighting the Germans at St. Mihiel and the Meuse-Argonne offensive. His unit was shelled relentlessly and was hit with mustard gas. In March, 1999, the French Government presented Ihringer with its highest recognition, The Chevalier of the Legion of Honor.

After the Armistice, Ihringer remained in Germany as part of the occupation force. A Bordulac native, he enlisted in the army in April, 1918, and was discharged the following June. During this time he missed the death of his father and the birth of his son.

The complete war story "Ole" Ihringer, as told by author Marvin Baker is expected to be released by Christmas 2000. Baker, senior news editor at the *Minot Daily News*, spent the fall of 1999 interviewing Ihringer. The book will be available in outlets across the state.

Giant turtles stand sentinel

Once upon a time, long ago, massive dinosaurs and twelve-foot crocodiles roamed parts of the state. Today, four humongous turtles stand sentinel in the Turtle Mountains! Ironically, three of them are named Tommy!

The odd named one of the bunch, the W'eel Turtle, doesn't take a back seat. Standing two-stories tall, this monstrous green beast hangs out in Dunseith and is touted to be the world's largest man-made turtle. It took George Gottbrecht 15 years of collecting to come up with the 2000 metal car wheels necessary to make the W'eel Turtle. Curt Halvorson, also of Dunseith, welded the wheels in place so the structure was ready for that community's centennial in 1982. Although this monstrous turtle is a bit clumsy looking, that's far from the case. It's one-ton head actually moves from side to side.

About 30 miles to the north in Boissevain, Manitoba, stands one of the Tommy Turtles. *Stands* is the appropriate verb because this big fellow has reared upon his legs to loom 22-feet above the neighboring park. Weighing five tons, Boissevain's tourist attraction holds a Canadian flag in one front foot and an American one in the other. Tommy doesn't just idly stand around either, he talks!

Back across the international border, Bottineau's Tommy Turtle sits atop a snowmobile. Local businesses took up the project and raised enough money so that birth was given to this massive three-ton turtle that promotes the area's winter attractions. Made in Wisconsin, the turtle was trucked to town during a stint of 20-below weather. It took three men three days to erect Tommy.

Finally there's the midget of the group, Belcourt's Tommy Turtle. This guy is just 9-and-a-half-feet long. Originally built to rest atop a float during a town parade, Tommy's final home is near that community's care center.

Although this little fellow doesn't talk and doesn't wave flags nor ride a snowmobile, he does outperform the much larger W'eel Turtle. Not only does the Belcourt turtle's head move, but so do his feet! Sorry, the tail is stationary.

Bottineau's Tommy Turtle sits atop a snowmobile to promote that area's winter attractions. Made in Wisconsin, this three-ton turtle was constructed during a three-day stint of 20-below weather.

The W'eel Turtle, above, impressively stands at the south entrance to Dunseith. It took 15 years to collect the 2000 metal car wheels that make up the world's largest man-made turtle.

Boissevain's Tommy Turtle, right, rears up on his hind feet greeting visitors with a Canadian flag in his right hand and an American flag in his left. He also talks!

Belcourt's Tommy Turtle is the smallest of the four sentinels. Originally built as part of a float, his current home is near that community's care center.

Petersburg

Guess who's coming to dinner?

The name Al Capone conjures up cigar smoking mobsters, tommy gun toting tough guys, gum chewing flappers, and the seedy districts of Chicago. You think of drive-by shootings, speakeasies, and get away cars. Nobody thinks about North Dakota with the mention of Capone's name. Except, that is, Stella O'Neil.

That's because it was in Petersburg, North Dakota, where Stella met a man she thinks was none other than this infamous mobster.

"It was a beautiful night. My best girlfriend and I were working in a restaurant owned by my folks," she said. "They came in wearing fine clothes to have dinner. They wanted the doors locked."

This didn't surprise Stella and her teenage friend, Agnes Asleson. Often people asked them to lock the doors for private parties. Besides, neither of the girls noticed the guards who went up the stairs between the restaurant and the hardware store to perch themselves on the diner's roof. They, also, didn't see the guard stationed outside the front door. Nor did they notice the fancy black cars with tinted glass that their guests drove into town. It wasn't until the next day that the girls learned about all this from startled residents. "Weren't you scared?" they asked.

They hadn't been scared. Because, inside the Hildre Café, everything went smoothly. The party used up two tables. One of them played popular tunes on the restaurant's piano. "We never heard it played that nice before," Stella said.

"They enjoyed our cooking. They couldn't get over how we two girls could cook the steaks," Stella said. "They were all very nice. This one, especially. I'm sure it was him (Capone). He was very nice to us. They just seemed like a group of people who came in for a good time."

Then, when the party decked out in high society garb left, they tipped the girls $5 apiece. That was a real shocker for the two high schoolers. If anyone even left a tip in those days, it'd be just a quarter or a box of candy. Five bucks was real money!

Of course, there's the question, where did that money come from?

Where's that sixth bandit?

Were there only five or was there a sixth man who pulled off the bullet riddled 1906 Sawyer bank robbery?

It was a cold October morning when a gang broke into Brassett and Lund's hardware store to grab guns and ammunition. Then they pillaged the Segerstrom store for general merchandise. After these successful heists, the now brazen bunch moseyed over to crack the safe at Sawyer's bank.

Dynamite was put in place to blow the safe door. Although the first charge awoke William Hodges who lived across the street in the post office building, it wasn't powerful enough to crack the safe.

Another charge was set off, then another. It wasn't until eight charges were set that the safe's door cracked open.

All this commotion awoke most of the town. Several locals grabbed rifles and shotguns and joined Hodges in the post office's second story. However, this fortification didn't go unnoticed. Three of the bandits, armed with Winchester rifles, stood guard outside the bank shooting at everything that moved. After several rounds of volley, a multitude of holes dotted the side of the post office building.

The barrage of bullets was so intense that others still en route to the scene were forced back to cover. Those in the building were pinned to the floor.

Oddly enough, no one was killed even though a piece of the safe's door was blown 250 feet across the street where it made a two-foot hole in the post office's second story wall.

On the way out of town, the gang, which some say had five members while others say six, left another barrage of fire. Shortly after, a posse was organized to head southwest along the Soo Line tracks.

Checking at every farmyard, they finally met a farmer who had talked with the desperadoes. He gave the first clear count of the men in the group that he suspected were hoboes. He said there were five.

After resting at his farm, three of them headed off to the southwest again while the other two headed northwest.

The two northwest bound fugitives, Jack Hayes and Charles Sullivan, were found sleeping in a haystack. They peacefully surrendered.

The other three, Mike "Dad" Duffy, E.G. Robinson, and Bert Conroy, were spotted walking the Soo Line tracks to Max. When ordered to stop, they took off. Robinson was brought down by a shot that broke his ankle. Conroy immediately surrendered by throwing up his hands sending money in all directions.

By jumping into a nearby swamp and only surfacing briefly for air, Dad Duffy eluded capture for another hour.

All five were sentenced to the state pen to serve terms of 14 years, 10 months to 20 years. Duffy never made it to the big house though. While in the Ward County jail, he passed out from what he called one of his spells and died 15 minutes later.

After impressing the judge about his feelings of contrition, Robinson received the lesser sentence. As it turned out, he was the only one of the four convicts who tried to escape from the pen. All four were released after serving seven to nine years.

What about that sixth man? Had there been another bandit who took off on his own? Those who said they saw six bandits, not five, leave town point to one more interesting fact. While housed in the Ward County jail, someone on the outside tried to saw through the bar windows of the gang's cell. Was this the sixth bandit? That's become one of North Dakota's unsolved mysteries.

Space coin

The NASA shuttle carried twelve 22-karat gold versions of the new dollar coin bearing the likeness of Sakakawea. The coins were part of the cargo in the July, 1999 flight which was the first space flight commanded by a woman, Eileen Collins.

The new golden colored dollar recently released by the U.S. Treasury features Sakakawea, the Indian woman who guided the Lewis and Clark expedition to the West Coast in 1805. Sakakawea was living at the Knife River Indian Villages when she joined the expedition.

For more information on Sakakawea, read *Dakota Mysteries & Oddities*.

Fort Ransom

The Vikings were here!

Did Vikings roam these parts hundreds if not thousands of years ago? Minnesota supporters of this notion point to the Kensington Runestone and various mooring stones as proof.

Some North Dakota lay historians claim Vikings docked in southeastern parts of the state and in the Turtle Mountains. Further, they contend that Pyramid Hill, which overlooks Ft. Ransom, was built by ancient mound builders 4000 years ago.

Geologists, on the other hand, contend the mound is nothing more than a natural hill cut into a conical shape by glacial erosion.

Then, a mile from that community, there's that unusual rock atop a hill overlooking Mooring Stone Pond. It's like the other boulders in the area except it's got a plus scratched in it with a three-and-a-half-inch hole marking its center.

Who would go to all the trouble to do this and why? Some say Vikings made that hole in the rock, then stuck a rod in it so they could moor their boats there during times when the Sheyenne River was much larger.

Again, most scientists don't agree. They ask, where are other Viking artifacts that support this theory? Surely, if the Vikings were here at one time, they would have left something behind other than just a hole in a rock!

Could a large boulder locals call Writing Rock be so easily dismissed? This large stone, also sitting atop this hill, is marked with parallel lines and dotted with circles. Geologists contend a glacier slowly moved pebbly grains of sand across this rock leaving a series of scratches and other marks. To substantiate this theory they point to similarly marked rocks found at the foot of glaciers in Alaska and Norway.

Two local lay historians spent their lives disputing this scientific explanation. Snorri Thorfinnson and A.Z. Nelson both contended the etchings were part of an alphabet with origins traceable to ancient China. Nelson theorized the bars (lines) represented years while the dots (circles) represented the number of people living in the valley at specific times.

So, what about the mooring stones? Could the markings on it, also, be as easily dismissed by scientists? Hardly.

Granted nature performs marvels, but is nature so precise it could etch a plus sign in a rock and, then, scratch out a three-and-a-half inch hole right in the center of that plus?

Let it be said that someone, sometime, somehow made that hole in that rock. It could have been Vikings mooring their boats. It could have, also, been Indians mooring their boats. One scientist contends the hole

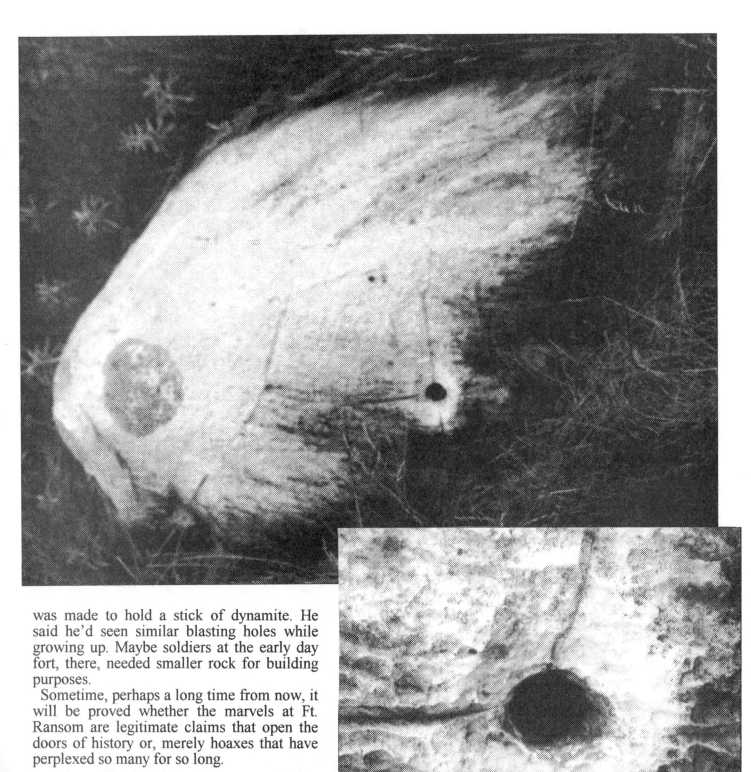

was made to hold a stick of dynamite. He said he'd seen similar blasting holes while growing up. Maybe soldiers at the early day fort, there, needed smaller rock for building purposes.

Sometime, perhaps a long time from now, it will be proved whether the marvels at Ft. Ransom are legitimate claims that open the doors of history or, merely hoaxes that have perplexed so many for so long.

This rock with a hole in it rests atop a hill overlooking what locals call Mooring Stone Pond. It's speculated when the Sheyenne River was much higher, Vikings moored their boats from a rod sticking out of the hole.
Inset, **notice the defined lines with the three-and-a-half inch deep hole in the middle. The size of the hole is larger than a quarter but smaller than a half dollar.**

Look closely to find parallel lines and dots on the flat surface of this rock located not far from Ft. Ransom. Could these markings be part of an ancient Sino-Tibetan alphabet indicating the origin of early day settlers? It's contended the lines stand for years with the dots indicating population. Geologists disagree with this interpretation. They say the markings are a phenomenon called chattermarks. As the ice of a glacier slides over a rock, some of the pebbles and sand grains it's carrying leave scratches and other marks. Note the carved initials, from a more modern time, on the high end of the rock.

Bismarck

Skyscraper of the Prairies

The 19-story North Dakota state capitol is sometimes referred to as the Skyscraper of the Prairies. Built out of natural materials like marble and brass, the white structure looms above Bismarck's northern horizon.

The first state capitol burned on December 28, 1930. With money scarce during the beginnings of the Great Depression, only two million dollars was allocated for the new building. That meant designers concentrated on efficient rather than ornate architecture.

Although Jamestown campaigned for the new structure, the people chose to build the state's *tallest* building in Bismarck.

Steele

World's Largest Sandhill Crane

New Salem has its Salem Sue, the world's largest Holstein Cow.
Wahpeton boasts the world's largest catfish, while Garrison sports the largest Walleye.
Nobody's arguing that Jamestown has the largest buffalo. It weighs in at 60 tons.
Then there's that giant grasshopper and those great big tin people on what's become known as the Enchanted Highway.
Don't forget all those really big turtles in Bottineau, Belcourt, and Turtle Lake not to mention the world's largest such reptile at Dunseith.
Have you seen all the giants in the state? Not unless you've seen the latest, Steele's 40-foot-tall sandhill crane.
Made of steel, local business owner Susie White hopes it's big enough and unique enough to pull you into town for a closer look.

Devils Lake

Devils Lake's sea monster?

Does a sea monster lurk beneath the waters of Devils Lake?

The February 5, 1886, issue of the *Devils Lake Inter-Ocean* newspaper recounts the legend of a monster rising from the depths of the lake to claim a band of Indians. According to the story, Chippewa braves were retreating across the waters after being defeated by victorious Sioux braves in one of numerous battles between the two. These braves were whisked away in a whirlpool when an immense turtle-like creature arose from the bottom of the lake.

The legend contends the creature laid across a subterranean passage. So, when it came ashore, water gushed into the uncovered tunnel.

On its way eastward toward Lake Wamduska, the monster's writhing body twisted off trees.

An 1800 sighting has the monster exiting Stump Lake and following the same trail it made earlier back to Devils Lake. *The commotion of the water, when it plunged into the lake. . .upset a number of canoes in which were many Sioux warriors, several of them being drowned.*

An article that, originally, appeared in the magazine section of the February 9, 1941, (Minneapolis) *Star Journal,* gave a different account of the monster's debut. Accordingly, Sioux braves had driven the Chippewa beyond their borders. While they were planning another attack, the Great Spirit Man, Owando the Seer, warned that if they did, a huge monster would arise from the lake and swallow them.

Undaunted, they began their trip. True to the warnings, the monster arose from the lake and swallowed most of the braves.

The Sioux, then, prepared to rendezvous with the monster. An ensuing whirlpool pitched Spirit Lake, one of their medicine men, into the waters. The braves found Spirit Lake who explained, while in the water, he found *the mouth of a subterranean passage connecting with an underground river that ran across the country to the Gulf of Mexico.*

And you thought there were only fish in Devils Lake!

The Bridges

Valley City is known as *The Bridge City*. This pictorial adds credence to that claim.

The ornate foot bridge, right, spans the Sheyenne River linking Valley City with its local college. Technically it's a three-span, 150 foot long suspension bridge, the only one of its kind in the state. Originally built in 1901 for less than $2000, the bridge had to be rebuilt in the early 1990s after someone drove his car over it. The cost was more than a quarter million dollars.

Valley City's 3,860 foot High-Line Bridge is one of the longest single track railroad bridges in the nation. The bridge links the prairie allowing trains to cross 162 feet above the Sheyenne River.

High-LIne Bridge was considered of such tactical importance that it was guarded during both world wars.

Rainbow Arch Bridge, above, is the only bridge in the state in which the concrete arches carry the weight. The bridge, built in 1925-26, spans 125 feet, arches 28 feet, and weighs over 1600 tons. Contractors skewed West City Park Bridge 25 degrees when they built it in 1929 to fit the river channel. The structure's twin, East City Park Bridge, was built four years earlier.

Want to know more about Valley City's unique bridges? Check out their web site at
http://www.hellovalley.com/valleycity/bridges/
or, better yet, drive to the community and take the town tour of eight scenic bridges.

The Old Can Pile

When Max Taubert built his gasoline station with the lunch counter that boasted four stools on the outskirts of Casselton in 1933, he called it "The Brick House." Located at the intersection of two highways next to the Great Northern Railway, the business capitalized on truckers, especially those hauling cattle to West Fargo.

Over the years, the station acquired a new moniker. People called the establishment *The Old Can Pile* because Taubert got into the habit of tossing empty oil cans into a pile fenced in by chicken wire. When the cans got to the top of the fence, he simply added more chicken wire. Eventually the structure topped 50 feet.

Thousands stopped by to see this tower of art and eat what was billed as the best hamburger served between Chicago and Seattle.

Taubert operated *The Old Can Pile* until he died in 1973. Wanting to keep this bit of local history alive, the owners of Loegering Manufacturing, the makers of tire crawler tracks, moved the tower 300 feet to make room for their plant. That's where the tower, painted silver and adorned with Christmas lights, stands today.

The Gray Lady of Sims

and other ghost stories

In 1923, Bertha Dordal, the wife of Rev. L.D. Dordal, died. Bertha had been sick for awhile when her sister came out to help. It wasn't long before death knocked at the parsonage where the Dordals lived next to the Sims Lutheran Church claiming the pastor's 26-year-old wife.

Somewhere along the line, Rev. Dordal married his deceased wife's sister and moved out of state.

No one reported hauntings at the small parsonage where the Dordals lived until the 1930s when stories ran rampant. There were claims the upstairs windows rose, then fell again as if someone was opening and closing them. However, when passersby looked, there was no one at the windows! Others watched the pump handle go up and down as if someone was trying to draw water even though no one was near the pump!

Most speculated the parsonage was haunted by Bertha Dordal, the only one known to have died there!

Sig Peterson, a local historian who grew up in the Sims-Almont area, believes the specter that's become known as the *Gray Lady of Sims* is a kind ghost. When he was little, he lived across the street and played with the Dordals' three children, Raymond, Harold, and Adeline.

Raymond and Harold became ministers. Peterson tells the story about a visit he had with Harold about 40 years ago. At that

time Harold was a pastor at a Moorhead College. Everyday several of the ministers got together for coffee. One morning, one of them told about his first call in western North Dakota when he had to leave the congregation on account of a ghost, that's when Harold told him the ghost was his mother!

Peterson, also, recalls when a girl stayed overnight at the parsonage with the family of the church's third minister. She slept upstairs. The next morning when the pastor's wife asked how she slept, she answered just fine. The only time she was disturbed, she said, was when the pastor's wife brought her a blanket. The pastor's wife responded that she hadn't brought her guest an extra blanket!

Then there are stories told by another minister's wife. Olga Nelson and her husband, Pastor Carl Gustav Nelson, lived in the parsonage for four years, from 1932 until 36. Although Olga died three years ago, her daughter Eunice remembers her mother talking about a ghost.

"My mother was as practical as anybody could be. Yet, she told these stories about the pump handle going up and down. . .I remember her saying she wasn't at all afraid. She was a friendly presence. Upstairs, my mother would see this gray shape. There would be breezes in the parsonage."

Wasn't that enough to scare the Nelsons away? "My mother would have been offended if she had moved away because of a ghost."

Others weren't so brave. The local story is that the church lost several ministers because their wives complained about a ghostly specter that haunted the parsonage. The congregation got so spooked, they sent a letter to the area bishop in 1938 complaining about ghostly activity.

Sig Peterson says he doesn't believe the Gray Lady haunts the abandoned parsonage anymore. He recalls a bachelor living there for 20 years and never being bothered.

Still, area ranchers, perhaps tongue-in-cheek, continue to blame the Gray Lady for things that go wrong. Who else could it be who unlocks their gates and lets their cattle out?

OTHER GHOST STORIES

Bismarck's phantom and goblin damned fairy

Two Bismarck officers - identified in the newspapers only as Scott and Stewart - watched as a female figure dressed in a white gown moved toward them from the opposite side of the street. The sighting was at two o'clock on an August morning in 1883. The officers were seated in front of Frank Frisby's drug store when they looked up Fourth Street and saw the apparition.

As reported in the *Bismarck Tribune*, Scott said to Stewart, "What is this coming in the middle of the street, at this time of night?" Then, when the figure reached the middle of the street, it vanished!

The paper reported: "The policemen hastened to the spot where the phantom appeared, and even examined the dust for foot prints. But nothing was found."

A few nights later, several Bismarck residents reported what they called "a goblin-damned fairy-moving object on Fourth Street." The *Tribune* reported the figure "walked over the hill on the sidewalk as silently as a stream of light or a falling feather. No sound of a footstep was heard and it glided along without a perceptible movement of the body." Then the man-like figure "vanished between the buildings."

No further sightings of these phantom specters were ever reported.

The ghosts at the governor's mansion

The archives at the State Historical Society in Bismarck include a report of a spirit haunting the former governor's residence. The story goes that Marion Burke, daughter of John Burke, said their butler, Tom Lee, only slept in the house when the governor's family was home. When they were away, he slept elsewhere. He, also, regularly locked the door to the basement stairs. The Burkes lived in the mansion from 1907 to 1912. It's been noted that one governor and a governor's secretary had died at the residence. The old governor's mansion is, now, a state historic site.

Flaxton's angry fiend

In February, 1928, a ghost reputedly threw stones, coal, and frozen potatoes about a room in the John Barker residence in Flaxton. Youngster Harlan Knight was in the room with Barker when these articles seemingly came out of the ceiling. Harlan ran and got his father who, then, witnessed the missiles. Residents searched the premises, but couldn't find the source of the spheroids, or, even a hole in the ceiling from which they could be flung.

State Historical Society of North Dakota

Did a spirit haunt the former governor's residence?

Hatton's ghostly organist

In the fall of 1897 two Hatton residents walking by their church around eight in the evening were surprised to hear music. The door of the church was closed, two of the windows were raised about five inches. Through the aperture they clearly heard soft music. They assumed someone was playing the organ. However, they wondered how they'd gained entry since the church was locked.

Three others came by and heard the music, too. The *Ransom County Gazette* reported: "The sounds are described to have been of a strange, weird character, and the stillness of the evening, the gathering gloom and the soft musical strains from the church produced a superstitious awe in the minds of the five men, and none of them cared to enter the church and investigate."

They sent for the preacher. Then the six of them entered the church, but they found no trace of the mysterious musician.

Devils Lake's phantom ship

In 1893 the *Devils Lake News* reported that Captain Heerman and six others saw a phantom ship in Devils Lake one morning around six. It reputedly came from Six Mile Bay and, then, sailed rapidly toward the narrows.

Coulee

Wedding ring found after 57 years

Greg Bommelman was feeding some geese near a watering hole on his property near Coulee when he caught the glimmer of a gold ring lying on the ground. Looking at the ring under a magnifying glass, Bommelman and Judie Hansen made out the engraved letters: H.C.R.

The letter "R" lit a light. About four years earlier, in 1996, the Rasmussen family from Kenmare had come out to the farm to search for a lost ring with a metal detector. It was in 1943 when Helen Rasmusson lost her ring while she was gardening.

Over the years she often searched for the ring that her husband, Tony, gave her when they were married in 1931. The searches stopped in 1971 when the couple sold their farm and moved to Kenmare.

Then, in 1996, a son from Wisconsin brought his metal detector along on a visit. Although they didn't find the ring, Bommelman remembered them looking for it when *he* found it.

In an interview in *The Kenmare News*, Helen said she'll wear the ring again. "It's too large now. I'll put it on a chain that I have with some birthstones. . .You can still see lines where the apple blossoms were engraved."

Unfortunately, Tony died in 1998. "I wish he was here to know the ring was found," Helen said.

Fingal

Leaning Tower of Fingal

Larry Steidl stands next to what has become known as the Leaning Tower of Fingal. During the wet spring of 1999, Steidl came home from the field one day to find his silo had tipped. He believes both the wet weather and some animal diggings under the silo's base contributed to the shift. At the time of this writing, Steidl was planning on a neighborhood party to bring the tower down safely. Until, then, it's heads up!

Grafton

40-years on the airwaves

"Did you hear about the two sows in the pasture? One said, 'Hey, have you heard from your boar friend lately?' The other one said, 'Yeah, I got a litter from him the other day!'" announces Uncle Sig over Grafton airwaves. Telling jokes like this is something the 90-year-old farmer's been doing for 40 years on KXPO radio.

Most would say his off-the-wall humor and ad lib commercials are way out of mainstream radio. They'd be right, he readily admits.

"I'm getting kind of old, now, and they think the dumb Polack doesn't know any better," Sig chuckles. "So, they figure, they might as well let me get away with it."

And get away with it he has to the delight of listeners from Winnipeg to Hillsboro, from Thief River Falls, Minnesota, to just east of Rugby and to the delight of advertisers who clamor to buy spots on his Sunday afternoon show, **Uncle Sig's Old Time Show**.

Sig Jagielski got his break in radio 40 years ago because he is Polish! Keeping up with listeners' requests, the station began playing some Polish tunes. However, no one at the station spoke the language. This meant a few songs with off-colored limericks were aired causing the phone lines to light up.

They called in Sig as a censor. Although he nixed the off-colored lyrics, he replaced them with salty comments that got the station's listeners buzzing. Uncle Sig was an instant success. It wasn't long before he was *king of the mike* on his own show.

Based on the popularity of the show, advertisers clamored to buy spots on the show. Were they in for a surprise!

Advertising on Uncle Sig's show was about as far removed from typical advertising as possible. Once Sig aired that a lot of stores were having sales. You know, buy one, get one free, he announced. They've got some mighty fine caskets at the funeral home. Maybe you should ask them if they'd give you one free if you bought one!, he punned.

Although the funeral director arched an eyebrow, he's still advertising with Sig to this day.

Then there's his famous toilet paper ad. "They've a real special on TP that'll come in handy when you use Ex-Lax," Sig matter-of-factly tells his audience.

Over the years the music on Sig's show changed from his original Polish songs to country and western music, waltzes and polkas. His program consists of music from his own collection of over 800 records, CDs, and tapes.

KXPO officials admit that many radio stations play old-time music, but, they say, only one station has Uncle Sig!

At his home, Uncle Sig stands by some of the clocks he's made as a new hobby.

Those county lines. . .

Remember Lehr's claim to fame that was told in the original *Dakota Mysteries & Oddities*? That community boasts it's the *Smallest City in the U.S.A. Situated in Two Counties*. That story got reader Neal Marrow thinking. When he grew up, he remembered part of his father's garage in Coulee was in one county while the other part was in another county. Coulee has less people than Lehr. So, wouldn't Coulee hold the title? Further research showed that Coulee is so small, it's not an incorporated city. So, Lehr still holds the claim. Checking further, Marrow learned that a double garage stands on that same spot today. And, yes, a structure on two sides of the county line pays proportional taxes to each county!

Opening school doors

The staff at the University of Minnesota told Anne Carlsen she should reconsider her decision to get a teaching degree. This wasn't the first time Carlsen had to fight for an education.

She hadn't been allowed to attend public school in Wisconsin until she was eight when a state psychologist approved her as *educable*. When they, finally, let her in the classroom, she completed her elementary studies in just four years!

Similarly, Carlsen shined in college, graduating with top honors in a class of 500. She went on to earn three more degrees including a doctorate in education.

Why, then, did all these educators discourage this bright, dedicated student from going to school?

The answer is because educators, despite the lessons they'd learned from Helen Keller, were still narrow minded about teaching the handicapped. They had a difficult time understanding how someone born with only stubs for arms and just one short deformed leg (which was later amputated) could fit into the system.

In a way, they were right. Carlsen had trouble finding a job especially since she entered the work force during the Depression. However, she persevered in her efforts. And she, eventually, succeeded big time.

Carlsen remembers employers turning her down time and again after she graduated from college. Once she applied for a job and was told she was too young. "But I'll get older," she answered. They countered she had no experience. "I'll get experience if I work," she said. Still, she didn't get the job.

She, finally, got work at the Crippled Children's School in Fargo. Although her pay was just $25 per month plus room and board, it was a job she kept until the school closed. She, then, worked a stint as a bedside instructor at a hospital in Minnesota.

When the Crippled Children's School reopened in Jamestown, she accepted another job with them. She taught there for many years then served as the school's principal and guidance counselor. In 1950, she was hired as their administrator, retiring in 1981. Upon her retirement, the school's name was changed, in her honor, to the Anne Carlson School.

Over the years Carlsen received many awards. She was named Handicapped American of the Year. The state gave her the Roughrider Award. The North Dakota Psychological Association named her psychologist of the year. Ironically, in 1980, the girl who was discouraged in her dream to become a teacher, was inducted into the National Teachers Hall of Fame!

State Historical Society of North Dakota

Dr. Anne continues to live in Jamestown. In an interview in the *Jamestown Sun*, she shared her philosophy: "All people deserve the same rights and privileges as other people . . .All people deserve to have an education geared to their ability level. . .to reach their potential. . .to develop their abilities."

290 miles to the gallon

Tired of driving a big car that gets poor gas mileage during a time of high gas prices? Ask West Fargo High School's welding class to build you a car. Their gasoline powered The Packer Bull got 290 miles to the gallon in competition with other gas misers. The only drawbacks, to get that kind of gas mileage, you have to coast a lot and your maximum speed is only 25 miles per hour.

A land of mystery and oddities

Within the borders of the state are the most fantastic badlands on earth. The magnificent display of erosion, right, was caused by the once rushing Little Missouri River. What the river and its tributaries left behind are deep gorges and spectacular valleys as well as an overview of the past. For miles around, the eroded sides of the buttes show the same layers meaning, several times over millions of years, this entire area was under water, the bottom of great inland seas. Each layer, then, indicates a specific time when waters covered the terrain.

The petrified forests found in the Badlands, also, point to invading seas. When trees died, perhaps because of high water, they soaked up the moisture. In that water were minerals. When the water evaporated and the wood of the tree rotted away, the minerals were left behind as a fingerprint.

Badland travelers marvel at the splendid array of color in the hills. Vibrant tones of red, yellow, and green cascade throughout the landscape. Take these colors out of their natural surroundings, though, and they pale, showing that all is relative.

Another oddity of relativity is that the colors change from season to season, from dry times to wet ones.

Among the red colors are scoria rock, actually clay baked into a brick with the burning of neighboring coal. Massive coal veins run about 30 feet below the surface in parts of the Badlands. It's expected exposed coal was, once, ignited by lightning strikes. The coal has been burning ever since.

This has created even another oddity, unique junipers that grow only in the Badlands. Here Rocky Mountain junipers grow in a slender, conical shape. Replant these trees anyplace else in the world, and they return to their typical spreading form! It's thought these trees grow in this somewhat stunted form because of pollutants given off by the burning coal veins.

Pictured on this page is another Badlands' marvel, the making of a cannon ball. Concretions are formed within rock like shale, clay, and sandstone by the collection of minerals around a core. The concretions get to be boulder-sized. As the softer soil erodes, round-shaped cannonballs are exposed. With more erosion, they tumble to the ground. Passersby wonder where that big, round rock came from? Who would have ever thought it could happen this way? Only nature!

Tioga

The beginning of the boom

Oil pumps, often called Grasshoppers, like the one above, dot parts of Western North Dakota. Left, a monument marks the location of the state's first oil well, the Clarence Iverson #1, near Tioga. In it's initial pumping on April 4, 1951, the well produced over 300 barrels of crude in 17 hours.

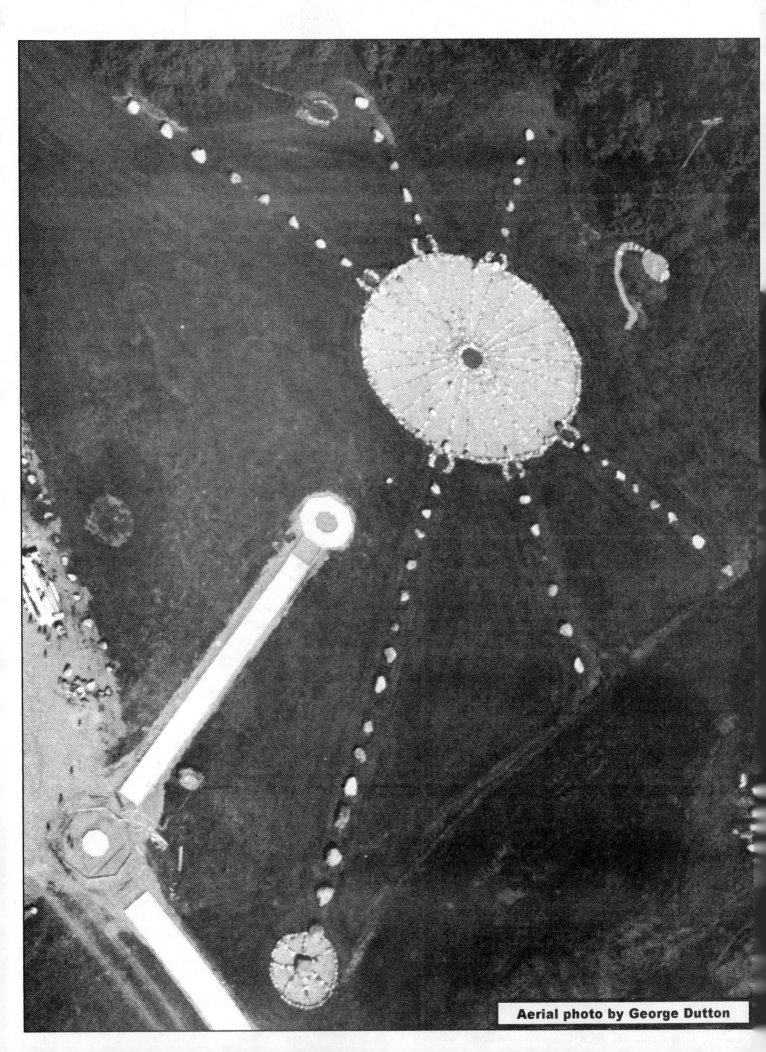

Aerial photo by George Dutton

Medicine Wheel Park

"I would like nothing better than to leave behind my own little cosmic joke on the face of the planet," Joe Stickler said in an interview with *The Forum* newspaper a couple of years ago.

For the past eight years, Stickler and his astronomy students have been building a massive solar calendar atop a large hill behind Valley City State University where he heads the science and math division.

Using locally gathered rocks and boulders, his students outlined a 68-foot diameter inner circle which represents the sun. Twenty-eight spokes, representing the number of days in the lunar cycle, radiate from this hub to a larger circle. This 213-foot circumference circle represents the Earth's orbit. Six of the 28 spokes extend past the wheel. These spokes are aligned to the sunrises and sunsets on the first days of each of the four seasons.

Stickler said the idea behind his Medicine Wheel was to build a solar calendar that reflects the spirit and purpose of approximately 100 such wheels found on the Great Plains and in the Rocky Mountains of the United States and Canada. Big Horn Medicine Wheel in northern Wyoming is this country's most well-known wheel. England's Stonehenge is the most well known in the world.

Stickler's model actually allows visitors to walk through the Solar System! Rocks representing the planets are spaced on a scale of one foot to 2,780,000 miles. Since the Earth's orbit corresponds to the outer circle, Mercury and Venus are found inside the circle with Mars just outside. The large rock located far away near the parking lot represents Jupiter. Even farther out are Saturn, Uranus, and Pluto.

Stickler stresses that Medicine Wheel Park is an astronomy lesson and isn't meant to attract cult worshipping.

However, he admits, there is something about the place that's spiritual. The wheel is about the earth, the sun, the moon, the planets, and the stars. "With a domain that size, things get spiritual," he says.

As far as his cosmic joke is concerned, Stickler didn't have to wait long to laugh. After word got out about Medicine Wheel Park, he's received correspondence from many regarding the *wheel's ancient origin*!

For more information on the internet:
http://medicinewheel.vcsu.edu

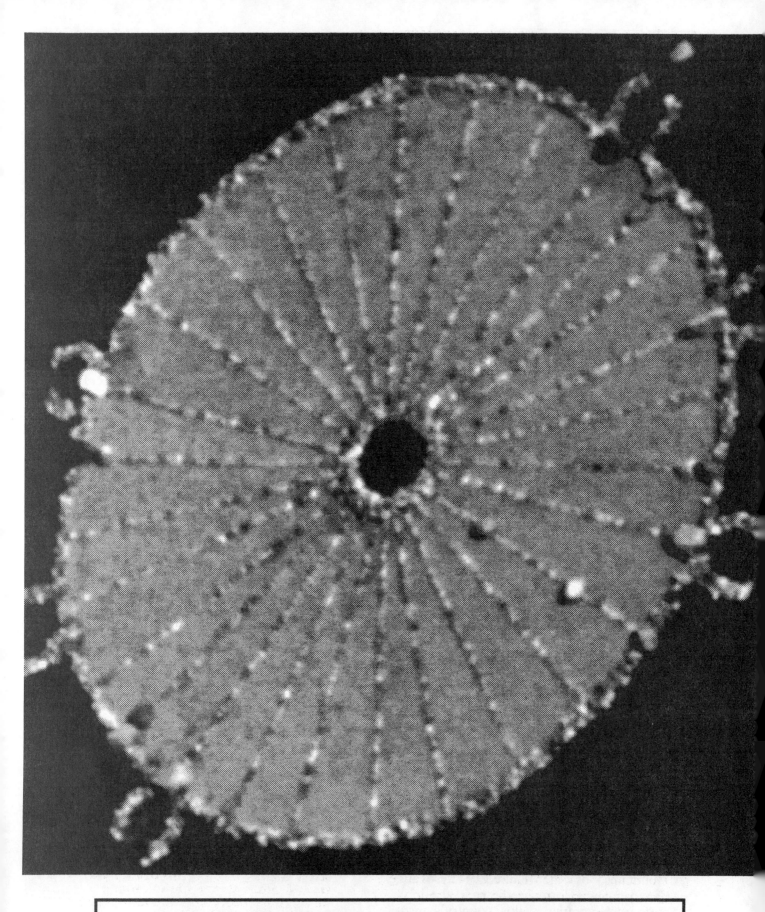

From overhead it looks like a giant Ferris Wheel!
This enlargement of the preceding aerial photo clearly shows the 28 lines
emanating from the inner circle (sun) to the outer circle (earth's orbit). People
flocked to see the Medicine Wheel. So, the city has turned that area into a park.
- Enhanced image from a photo by George Dutton

How to Use the Medicine Wheel as a Calendar

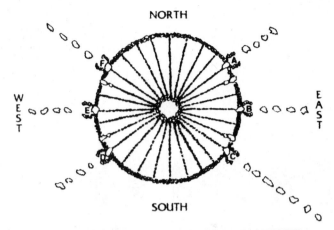

NORTH

WEST

EAST

SOUTH

1st Day of Season	Sunset Position	Sunrise Position
Summer	C	D
Fall	B	E
Winter	A	F
Spring	B	E

The Medicine Wheel functions as a natural calendar using six long external spokes as "sight lines" which point to the horizon positions of the rising and setting Sun at the beginning of each season. For example, by standing at the rim of the Wheel in the small rock cairn (marked C in the above graphic) and looking across the Wheel through the center along the extended spoke, one can see the point on the distant western horizon where the sun will set on the first day of Summer. The Table below indicates the positions for observing the sunrise and sunset alignments on the first day of each of the seasons.

By walking from "Winter solstice sunset position A" to "Summer solstice sunset position C," the 72 degree annual panoramic sweep of the sun's setting positions on the western horizon can be surveyed. Community gatherings to observe and celebrate sunrises and sunsets on the first day of each season are sometimes scheduled.

- from a Valley City State University pamphlet

DAKOTA TRIVIA

NAMED AFTER A JAPANESE GENERAL
The small town of Kuroki, located between Antler and Westhope was named after Itei Kuroki, the Japanese general who defeated the Russians during the Ruso-Japanese War of 1904-05. The town was founded in 1905, the year Kuroki visited the United States. In 1920 the small community boasted a population of 20!

CENTURY'S FIRST BABY
Emily Elizabeth Nyhof was, officially, the first baby born in the state in the 21st Century.* Emily was born at 1:12 a.m. on New Year's Day 2000 in Fargo. The family lives in West Fargo.
  *Some consider the 21st Century as beginning on January 1, 2001

LINDBURG LANDED IN FARGO
Charles Lindburg landed his plane, the *Spirit of St. Louis*, in Fargo on August 26, 1927, as part of a national tour of 82 cities. Lindbergh gained worldwide fame by soloing from New York to Paris just three months earlier.

HOW DID THE KODAK CAMERA GET ITS NAME?
The Kodak camera was named after its inventor, David Henderson Houston, scrambled the letters of the word Dakota. To make a good sounding word, Houston added an extra K. Houston was a Red River Valley farmer who patented his camera in 1887 and, then, sold the rights to George Eastman.

SHORT-LIVED
Dedicated in October, 1974, the multi-million dollar anti-ballistic missile system near Nekoma was shut down four months later because it was considered out-of-date. The complex contained 30 Spartan long-range and 60 Sprint short-range missiles.
See related story in this book

ONLINE WEDDING
After talking to an internet pen pal from Chile, a Grand Forks couple decided to marry online. Norm Reich and Kristina Phelps designed their own web site to broadcast their April 29, 2000 wedding.

Medora

North Dakota's Napoleon?

Three men carrying repeaters approached a man armed with only a single shot rifle. When the dust lifted from this 1883 skirmish, one of the attackers was dead, another had a broken leg, and the third surrendered. How could this be? It was because the man they had chosen to run out of the North Dakota Badlands was no ordinary man. He was the Marquis de Mores. A man some say was born to fight!

The Marquis was born Antoine-Amedee-Marie-Vincent-Amat Manca de Vallombrosa in Paris on June 14, 1858. Born during a time of turbulence, he glorified the era of his childhood. It was during this time that Napoleon Bonaparte's nephew attempted to revive his uncle's empire. Napoleon III wrote treatises and circulated pamphlets outlining his social reforms. He was a political liberal and a proponent of agricultural and industrial development. Twice Napoleon III failed to overthrow King Louis Phillippe.

The Marquis, too, purported grandiose political and economic schemes to thwart the growth of the British Empire and to oust the Jews from political power within France. Some even contend that all the Marquis' scheming was to ultimately enable him to become emperor!

Growing up an aristocrat, Antoine learned to speak English, German, and Italian. After receiving a degree at a Jesuit College, he studied military training at Saint-Cyr. He joined France's regular army only to resign as a lieutenant during the peacetime of 1881. He considered his position too dull. That year, the man now titled the Marquis de Mores, plunged his efforts into stock market speculation, an activity that had become popular among young aristocrats. Like so many others, he lost money. Estimates place his losses at over $100,000, a debt satisfied by his father.

While dabbling in the stock market, he met Medora von Hoffman, a stunning American socialite who was visiting Paris. They married on February 15, 1882. Medora's Wall Street banker father, Louis von Hoffman, gave the Marquis a $3 million wedding gift. After the honeymoon, the couple moved to New York City where

The Marquis de Mores was an imposing figure astride his horse. He not only fit in but blossomed in the Dakota Badlands. However, he had problems in his dealing with the locals.

State Historical Society of North Dakota photo

the Marquis worked as an officer in his father-in-law's bank. The couple electrified New York's socialites. Much to his liking, the Marquis' caesar-like schemes captivated East Coast financiers. Of particular interest was his scheme to raise cattle in the West, slaughter them on site, and, then, ship them by rail to market. This way hotels in Bismarck and Fargo could buy their steaks locally instead of buying the meat of Montana steers that were shipped to Chicago where they were slaughtered and dressed. Markets could be developed in the East for lower priced steak because of inherently lower costs. Shipping slaughtered meat was cheaper than shipping live cattle because only about 40% of the animals are used as meat. Additionally, cattle lose weight when shipped, and their bodies are often bruised. Also, the plan called for less middlemen. The *Call of the West* where the Marquis could implement his plan soon outweighed the tedious doldrums of banking. In 1883, the Marquis, along with his secretary, arrived at the banks where the Little Missouri River and the Northern Pacific Railroad met. A small town called Little Missouri already existed at that crossing. The Marquis decided to build a 26-room chateau across the river, on the west bank, and rename the community which boomed, Medora, to honor his wife. The Marquis adored the Badland's unusual buttes and valleys, startling color contrasts, and petrified wood. An avid hunter, he cherished the area's mountain sheep, black and while-tailed deer and beaver. Businesswise, the location was closer to markets than Montana. The river provided plenty of water, and the valleys offered shelter for cattle. To the Marquis, there was no better place to build his slaughterhouse

Although the Marquise was an elegant woman from the East, she blended with the rugged western lifestyle. People adored her. On the one hand, she entertained in elegant style. On the other, she went on hunting trips to Montana.
State Historical Society of North Dakota photo

- State Historical Society of North Dakota photo

The Marquis' packing plant was massive. All that remains, today, is the smokestack.

than at the junction of the Northern Pacific Railroad with the Little Missouri River.

Within three months, the Marquis owned more land than any area rancher. That grated on some local ranchers. When he began fencing this land, that angered more of them. Fencing was against the customs of the wild west. Some regarded it as a way to control all the water rights. Talk ran rampant about what that *crazy* Frenchman would do next!

Malicious talk turned to hostility. The Marquis claimed he was shot at 18 times. The most known of these incidents was when he shot back killing buffalo hunter William Luffsey. This was just three months after the Marquis had come to the Badlands.

Years after the incident, Edward Allen, one of the lawyers who defended the Marquis, said the fencing of the vast ranch in Billings County led to the enmity of neighboring ranchers. They employed three *bad men* to frighten the interloping Frenchman out of the country.

Allen said when the three hired guns came across the lone Marquis, they encountered trouble they hadn't expected. He said all three had repeaters while the Marquis only sported a single-shot rifle. Nevertheless, the Marquis killed one of the men, killed two horses, broke one man's leg, and arrested the third.

The Marquis' version, as told at his trial, was a little different. He said he and Frank Miller were attacked by O'Donald, Luffsey, and Reuter. He said Luffsey was killed in the five-minute ruckus. However, he said he didn't know whose gun fired the lethal bullet.

O'Donald, the man considered to be the leader, denied there was a plot to scare the Marquis out of the country. He said they were riding along, minding their own business, when someone unknown began shooting at them. He said the first shot knocked his gun out of his hand. Then, another, went through his thigh and killed his horse. He said he and Reuter retreated only to be fired on again.

An interesting note is that when asked at the trial if the Marquis had ever killed anyone, he admitted to killing two men in duels in France.

Although acquitted, the shooting took its toll on the Marquis. Two hearings, a grand jury inquiry, and a trial took time away from his business for the next two years. East Coast financiers became skittish about financing an operation run by someone so notorious. In the Badlands, public sentiment soured even more toward a man who had killed someone locals regarded as one of their own. Add to this the staggering expense of legal defense.

Nonetheless, the Marquis managed to build his Medora business operations. In 1884, he grazed 5000 head of cattle and sheared 14,000 sheep. He actually shipped beef to Chicago and Baltimore that year.

103

He started a stage line to Deadwood to accommodate those en route to the gold rush. He founded the Northern Pacific Refrigerator Car Company and began a salmon shipping business from Portland, Oregon to New York. He even financed *The Badlands Cowboy*, Medora's local newspaper.

1884 was, also, a banner year for the town of Medora. Two-hundred-fifty people now lived in a town boasting a few main street businesses, three hotels, several saloons, a church, and a brickyard.

On July 4, 1886, Medora celebrated an historic milestone as the first car of butchered beef was shipped to New York. Plans had been laid to market what was referred to as *range to table beef* at shops in the tenement districts as well as at a market for aristocrats on Broadway.

Sales faired well at first. However, there wasn't money to be made in the tenement

The Chateau de Mores as it is today. The Marquis loved the rugged beauty of the Badlands in the background.

State Historical Society of North Dakota photo

districts because those shoppers, lacking refrigeration, could only buy daily amounts. The beef was well received at restaurants aimed at the wealthy until the newness wore thin. Diners, then, returned to ordering their customary corn fed beef. In short order, seeming successful markets in Baltimore and New York fizzled. The fledgling enterprise was, also, beset by a new factor in the business equation. The railroads gave freight rebates to Chicago packers enabling them to undersell Medora beef in key markets.

Beset by estimated losses of between three-hundred thousand and two million dollars, the Marquis' plans to enter the entrepreneurial ranks of J.P. Morgan and J.J. Hill, also, fizzled. Louis von Hoffman bailed out his son-in-law.

Also ended was what Edward Allen called the Marquis' stepping stone to become the Emperor of France. Allen contended the Marquis wanted his beef scheme to turn millions into billions so he could return to France, corrupt the French army, and ultimately establish himself as emperor.

In the fall of 1886, the de Mores family gave up the beef business and returned to New York. The following year, they went to France. After bagging tigers on a hunt in Nepal, the couple returned by boat to the Marquis' homeland. It was on that return trip that the Marquis excitedly plotted what would become his next scheme, running a railroad into the heart of China. The idea was to build the only railroad from Tonkin (North Vietnam) into the heart of China. This *scheme of global proportions* appealed to many in France because it allowed quicker trade with China.

The Marquis proposed a two-stage plan. First he wanted to build a railroad from the Gulf of Tonkin to north of Haiphong. The track would later be expanded into the Chinese mainland.

The tempo became so positive the Marquis personally invested several thousand dollars into the project in anticipation of government backing. However, the plan was squashed under the thumb of Ernest Constans, France's minister of interior.

The Marquis lashed back. He returned to France where he publicly criticized Constans whom he considered a Jew with intentions of destroying France's internal government. He bought a line of newspapers in which he purported socialism and attacked the Jews and the British. His papers exposed government graft and promoted programs for the underprivileged.

The Marquis' anti-Semitic stands gained him a strong following. It, also, made him a lot of enemies. Constans had him arrested. With a force of 300, Constans interrupted a political meeting of the Marquis and 200 of his supporters. Since Constans' group carried sticks, the Marquis pulled a revolver for protection. He was arrested and held on charges of being an accomplice in a murder attempt of a police agent. If convicted, it could have meant the death penalty.

Although a lot of political pressure was put on the courts, the attempted murder charges were dismissed, and the Marquis was fined $20 for carrying a concealed weapon.

The following year, after losing an election as an anti-Semite candidate for the Paris council, the Marquis was, again, tried. June 4, 1890, newspaper accounts read: "Paris is looking forward to a sensation in the trial of Marquis de Mores. From intimations which have leaked out of the official channels of information, it is expected that the remarkable history of the Marquis will not only be retold but with new and startling revelations as to his connection with anarchistic and other revolutionary conspiracies."

- State Historical Society of North Dakota photo

An early day photo of Medora. Look closely and you'll see a cow walking next to the boardwalk.

Most of the article was political propaganda. Although the Marquis consorted with anarchists, most historians believe he was a nationalist. He did not purport revolution to end government but to change government. The serious charges were dropped, and he served three months in jail for organizing an illegal assembly.

During these tumultuous years in France, the Marquis participated in several duels. One newspaper account credited him with battling in over 20 duels, killing many of his opponents. Twice his dueling caught the press' attention. There was a duel after Jewish editor, Camille Dreyfus, criticized the Marquis in *La Nation*. After volleying shots, Dreyfus fell to the ground. However, his wound wasn't fatal.

It was a later duel that damaged the Marquis' political popularity. Although Joseph Myer, a Jewish officer, was a noted army swordsman, he fell victim to the Marquis' blade. Some said the Marquis got a drop during an unguarded moment. Myer's death resulted in another trial. Again the Marquis was acquitted.

The Marquis took his causes to Africa. Here he promoted another scheme, a Franco-Islamic alliance against the Jews and the British. He was concerned about Britain's growing prominence on the Dark Continent.

The 38-year-old Marquis was murdered by some of his escorts while crossing the Sahara Desert. For two hours the wounded man gallantly fought off his attackers. Rumor about his death spread throughout the world. Some claimed he was the victim of a British conspiracy. Others blamed his death on an influential Jewish mercantile family. Some thought the Marquis met his fate at the hands of enemies within the French government. Then there were those who contended he was just killed by thieves.

A month later, over ten thousand packed the streets of Paris for the Marquis' funeral. After laying her beloved to rest, the Marquise offered a reward and financed a private investigation. "It was characteristic of his devoted and high spirited Marquise that she should go to Africa to hunt down the slayer of her husband," one newspaper reported.

Two years later, three Tourareg natives were arrested for the murder. One died while waiting trial. The second was sentenced to twenty years hard labor. The third was given the death sentence. At the Marquise's pleadings, the death sentence was reduced to hard labor for life. She said she wanted to be more merciful to the killers than they had been to her husband.

About the author. . .

More Dakota Mysteries & Oddities is William 'Jack' Jackson's third book. His first book *North Country Jack's Almanac*, a collection of Minnesota folk stories, was published in 1980. His second book, *Dakota Mysteries & Oddities*, sold 5000 copies in just four months after it hit the stands last September.

Ever since Jackson was a kid, he's enjoyed the odd and the unusual. He remembers sitting with his father on their front porch when the evening paper was delivered. While his dad read all the interesting news, "Billy" as he was called, then, gleaned the paper for those little cartoon features with unusual tidbits. "I'd rather know how many words there are that are spelled the same forwards or backwards, than the progress of warring factions in the Middle East," Jackson says.

Although he's over 50, now, and, over the years, the writer of some of the state's most provocative investigative journalism articles, Jackson still enjoys sitting in his chair reading trivia.

He's fine-tuned this hobby into storytelling. If you give him an off-the-wall fact, don't be surprised if he turns it into a feature story!

Jackson was lucky to find his second wife, Arlyce, in a small North Dakota town. She shares his adventurous spirit of traveling the countryside. Together they've been to over 400 North Dakota communities. Their dream is to visit every town in the state.

For the last few years, their four-year-old daughter, Eden, has traveled with them. She's attended an open legislative session. She sat on Ft. Ransom's Writing Rock. She stood on, but was not allowed to enter, Starkweather's so-called Back-Door-To-Hell vault. When they took her, as a toddler, to see Alkabo's Writing Rock, she sneaked in past the iron bars guarding the stones so she could *touch the drawings*. Seems like fascination with the mysterious and odd is a family thing with the Jacksons.

LOOK FOR UPCOMING BOOKS
by Wm. JACKSON

Order the *original* Dakota Mysteries & Odditites™

Did you know the first fight between a UFO and a fighter aircraft happened in North Dakota skies?

It was in 1948 when a P51 World War II Mustang took on what the pilot claimed was a UFO. A ground controller watched the plane attack what he thought was a bright light.

Although the plane revved to over 400 miles per hour, the object easily sped away.

UFO or hoax? Read the details of this amazing story in **DAKOTA MYSTERIES & ODDITIES™**.

You'll, also, learn who the North Dakotan was who is credited as being the man who started the Flying Sauger Age in 1947. While commercially flying near Mt. Rainier, this pilot saw a chain of nine saucer-shaped objects at 9500 feet. He estimated they were traveling over 1600 miles per hour. Machines from outer space? Not according to the pilot. He theorized the flying saucers were actually. . . read the book!

Jim Altner got away with double murder near Bowbells in 1958. Yet, today, he has the dubious distinction of being the existing inmate who's served the most time in the state pen. Why did he turn himself in? Read the book!

Life ended for Sophia Eberlein when her second husband bludgeoned her to death with a hammer in 1931. Some contend Sophie still lives on earth as a ghost in the Harvey library which was built where her home once stood. Before you shrug this story off as poppycock, read the book!

Could a mound located near Fort Ransom in the southeastern part of the state actually be a pyramid that precedes the Egyptian tombs? Some lay historians claim what has become known as Pyramid Hill was built by ancients 4000 years ago. You'll find exciting details in **DAKOTA MYSTERIES & ODDITIES™**.

Investigative reporter Jack Jackson crisscrossed the state the last few years to find these unusual stories.

A few minutes after midnight, Ole Abelseth was awakened by a noise. The noise was the Titantic hitting an iceberg! Learn how this young Dakota man survived the sinking of the unsinkable ship, and why his parents weren't aboard the doomed vessel. It's all in the book!

In 1966, Clayton Weedeman read his obituary in the paper. This one-time Parshall farmer learned he'd died in a motel fire. He decided to go on the lamb and evaded authorities for 13 years until a dogged detective from. . .the rest of the story is in the book!

As odd as it seems, the man who invented modern day downhill skiing is buried in the relatively flat terrain of a cemetery near his Denbigh homestead. How did this famed Norwegian end up in North Dakota? His story is found in the book.

Imagine standing on the shores of a large inland sea watching steam rise as volcanoes spew molten lava into the waters. Imagine standing on the foothills of a massive mountain range with rocky cliffs majestically jutting into the skies. You couldn't be standing in North Dakota unless, that is, you turned back time. Since you can't do that, turn the pages of **DAKOTA MYSTERIES & ODDITIES™** to relive this bygone era.

On June 20, 1957, a tornado ripped a 100 block swath of destruction through one of Fargo's residential districts, killing ten and injuring 103. Before the 1500-foot-wide funnel spun itself out, it traveled over 27 miles. During that storm, a seven-month-old baby was whisked from his mother's arms and carried away in a swirl of debris. Did rescue workers find the baby alive or dead? The answer is in the book.

Kidnapping is rare in the relatively crime-free state of North Dakota. That is except for the eight kidnappings that happened during a hot 18-month period in. . .read the book!

If you like the mysteries on television's *Unsolved Mysteries* or the investigations on *Dateline*, you're going to love **DAKOTA MYSTERIES & ODDITIES™**.

You've read the sequel, now read the original.

To place your order, just call 1-800-277-2454. Be sure to ask for an autographed copy.

Dakota Mysteries & Oddities is a registered trademark.

1-800-277-2454